The Teaching of Ka

This book tells the story of teaching Kathakali, a seventeenth-century Indian dance-drama, to contemporary performers in Australia.

Rigorous analysis and detailed documentation of the teaching of multiple learners in Melbourne, both in the group workshop mode and one-on-one, combined with the author's ethnographic research in India, lead to a unique insight into what the author argues persuasively lies at the heart of the art's aesthetic – a practical realisation of the theory of *rasa* as first articulated in the ancient Sanskrit treatise on drama *The Natyashastra*. The research references the latest discoveries in neuroscience on "mirror neurons" and argues for a reconceptualisation of Kathakali's imitative methodology, advancing it from the reductive category of "mimicry" to a more contemporary and complex mirroring, which is where its value lies in Australian/intercultural actor performer training.

The Teaching of Kathakali in Australia will be of great interest to students and scholars of theatre and dance, intercultural actor training, practice-led research and interdisciplinary studies of neuroscience and performance.

Arjun Raina was trained as an actor at The London Academy of Music and Dramatic Art and as a Kathakali dancer at the International Centre for Kathakali, New Delhi, India. He has been performing and teaching drama and theatre for over 30 years. Arjun holds a PhD in Theatre and Performance from Flinders University, Australia, and has taught at the National School of Drama, New Delhi, and at Ambedkar University and Ashoka University, both in India.

Routledge Advances in Theatre and Performance Studies

For more information about this series, please visit: https://www.routledge.com/
Routledge-Advances-in-Theatre--Performance-Studies/book-series/RATPS

The Teaching of Kathakali in Australia

Mirroring the Master

Arjun Raina

LONDON AND NEW YORK

First published 2021
by Routledge
2 Park Square, Milton Park, Abingdon, Oxon OX14 4RN

and by Routledge
52 Vanderbilt Avenue, New York, NY 10017

Routledge is an imprint of the Taylor & Francis Group, an informa business

British Library Cataloguing-in-Publication Data
A catalogue record for this book is available from the British Library

Library of Congress Cataloging-in-Publication Data
A catalog record has been requested for this book

ISBN: 9780367539962 (hbk)
ISBN: 9781003084105 (ebk)

Typeset in Times
by Deanta Global Publishing Services, Chennai, India

Contents

1 Mirroring not mimicking the master

In a traditional Kathakali performance, when, after finishing his makeup and costuming, a Kathakali actor looks into a mirror, he sees looking back at him the precise image of a god, a demon, an epic hero or heroine. This specific image or social presence has taken the performer four hours to create, and six to eight years of actor training to embody (Figure 1.1). The performer has learnt this art from a *guru* or a master practitioner. He has worked for years as a *shishya* or disciple observing his *guru* while imitating his actions. This observation and imitation of a *guru* is central to Kathakali actor training.

In an introductory Kathakali actor-training workshop conducted in Melbourne, a student actor asked if the practice of a Kathakali actor was similar to that of a Filipino impersonator of a famous performer like Elvis Presley. To him, both seemed similar forms of mimicry. A consequent reading of academic literature on Kathakali offered the repeated use of the word mimicry to describe its teaching methodology.

In India, a traditional Kathakali teacher has no need to explain Kathakali's imitative pedagogy to a learner. Imitating a master practitioner is an accepted part of traditional Indian dance and acting culture. On the other hand, in Australia, explaining what Kathakali is, and how it is taught, is a performative act, in the English language. While communicating in English with learners, I, a Kathakali teacher, found asking learners to mimic me not a very accurate word for the act of imitating me. In the same introductory workshop in Melbourne, when an actor did actually mimic me, and imitated and repeated what looked to me like a generalised and artificial version of my action, I found it inappropriate to ask for an improved, or a more precise mimicry of my action. Even a request for a more specific imitation felt inadequate. In contemporary western culture, to mimic or to imitate someone is not considered high art. Drama schools in Australia, for example, follow the western pedagogy of encouraging actors to interpret and improvise both text and character, while individualising their creative interpretations. In contrast, Kathakali actor training (Zarrilli 1984, 1992, 2000a, 2000b, 2004, 2009, 2011; Zarrilli et al. 2013) works itself through a teacher-led program of imitative learning, preparing the learner to embody archetypical characters. As a Kathakali performer and teacher, my own experience of Kathakali actor training suggests a more complex and nuanced "mirroring" than a reductive mimicking by the learner of the teacher's actions. By "mirroring" I refer not to the inversion of an image in the mirror, but to the functional value of "mirror neurons" within the mirror neuron system in

Figure 1.1 Made-up, costumed and ready for performance: Hanuman the monkey god (Madavoor Vasudevan Nair). (Photo courtesy of Sreenath Narayan.)

the human brain. The latest research in neuroscience on mirror neurons[1] (Gallese 2003, 2009; Gallese and Sinigaglia 2011; Gallese et al. 1996) suggests a deeper evolutionary link between the act of observing and doing.[2] It is through a sustained

---

1   This "mirroring," as defined by the linkage of the act of observation with that of doing, is different to the traditional usage of mirroring in contemporary theatre training wherein one participant mirrors the action of the other, i.e., the right hand of one imitates the left hand of the other.

2   Recent excitement in the field of neuroscience suggests there exists a "mirror mechanism" in the human brain supporting the intersubjectivity involved, for example, in the intimate social interaction as in the mirroring process, i.e., the mirroring by a learner of a teacher's actions. This intersubjectivity the mirroring mechanism mediates by integrating the act of observing with the act of doing, "[m]irror Neurons are premotor neurons that fire both when an action is executed and when it is observed being performed by someone else" (Gallese 2009:520).

mirroring, then, of the Kathakali *guru* or master that a student receives what I argue for throughout this book as the central offering in this intercultural exercise, i.e., the performer's *rasa* or taste of aesthetic pleasure. This book documents and shares the process of this transfer of *rasa* from master to disciple locating the research exercise primarily in Melbourne, Australia, where the author now lives.

Over the past four centuries, Kathakali has been taught both in the group class-room teaching mode, with the teacher present with other singers and musicians, and in the more private one-on-one space, often in the teacher's home. This book works primarily with the one-on-one space. In the Kathakali one-on-one teaching space, the teacher repeatedly demonstrates the actions to be learnt while sing-ing the text and keeping rhythm or *tala* with a wooden stick, beating time on a wooden stool. The student dancer-actor learns the dramatic actions by imitat-ing the teacher's demonstrations of these actions. This includes embodying and illustrating with hand gestures the sung text, as well as imitating the embodied dance choreography. The learner embodies the song, allowing the *bhava* or the emotional state that exists in the song to inspire and possess him. The teacher expresses the *bhava* through singing the text or *padam*, keeping rhythm through-out the performance with the rhythm stick or *taalam*. The dancer-actor expresses the *bhava* through an enactment of the *padams* interspersed with pure dance pieces or *kalaashams*. This stage action is then received, realised and appreci-ated by the audience as an embodied emotional experience of aesthetic pleasure or *rasa*[3] (Pollock 2016; Krishnamoorthy 1979; Kumar 2010; Vatsyayan 2008; Shwartz 2006).

Kathakali actor training: key aesthetic features

Kathakali actor training is based on foundational principles of Indian aesthet-ics that guide the four key elements of an actor's representation: *angika* or body; *vacika* or speech; *aharya* or costumes; and *satvik* or the inner emotional. Kathakali's performance culture includes all four kinds of *abhinayas* or expres-sions of the act of performance, features found in all so-called "traditional" Indian dance-drama forms. These include *angika abhinaya*, the art of enactment relat-ing to the movement of the *anga* or limbs including hand gestures and facial expressions; *vachika abhinaya* or the art of the spoken word or, as is the case with Kathakali, the sung text; *aharya abhinaya* or the expressing of character and mood and feeling though elaborate costuming and makeup; and finally *satvik abhinaya* or the art of expressing the inner emotional world of the characters. All these four forms of *abhinaya* commune with each other, offering for the viewer

---

3 According to the Indian aesthetician Pravas Jivan Chaudhury, *rasa* is "originally a physiological term and figures in the medical literature (Ayurveda) of India. It means the physical quality of taste, and also any one of the six tastes, vis. sweet, acid, salt, bitter, astringent and insipid" (1956:219). *Rasa* in the present context is then a "taste" of aesthetic pleasure.

Figure 1.2 Pachcha (green) Divine Kingly character (Kalamandalam Gopi). (Photo courtesy of Sreenath Narayan.)

or audience an aesthetic experience defined traditionally as *rasa* or a taste of aesthetic pleasure (Figure 1.2).

Rasa theory in Indian aesthetic explores the place of emotion in art. For more than a thousand years, Indian intellectuals have debated the location of emotion in art. Does emotion exist primarily in the poet or writer, in the character or text, in the artistic object on stage, or does it exist in the audience? *Rasa*, or a taste of aesthetic pleasure, suggests both that which is tasted and that which tastes. In drama, is the dramatic poet or writer the first taster of the emotion or is a taste of *rasa* reserved for the audience? This book engages with these traditional ideas of *rasa* while attending to a significant gap in *rasa* scholarship, offering the neglected experience of the performer's body and its pleasure as another vector in the *rasa* debate. Through the bodies of the master practitioner and disciple, and through an appreciation of their pleasures, the one-on-one site of Kathakali actor training offers an opportunity to engage with and nuance the traditional understanding of *rasa*.

A key concept extending *rasa* into the realm of actor training is *rasaabhinaya*. In Kathakali, the training of embodied emotional states or *bhavas* is called *rasaabhinaya*. There are nine *bhavas*, namely *shringar* (desire), *hasya* (laughter), *karuna* (sadness), *raudra* (rage), *veera* (heroic), *bhayanaka* (fear), *vibhats* (disgust), *adbhuta* (wonder) and *shanta* (peace). The actor is trained to embody these formal emotional states not only through facial expressions, but even through a preparation of the entire body. Traditional scholarship on Indian aesthetics has *bhava* as the actor's embodiment of emotion and *rasa* as the audience's taste of aesthetic pleasure. The term *rasaabhinaya* sets up a contradiction, suggesting as it does the actor's tasting of aesthetic pleasure. This book works to negotiate and resolve this contradiction, offering evidence to suggest that the performer too tastes aesthetic pleasure or *rasa*.

The sociopsychophysical and "the old social" in Kathakali training

Over the last century, a large number of western practitioners have been influenced by non-western[4] processes of actor training inspired by the work of Russian acting teacher Konstantin Stanislavsky, one of the first western practitioners to engage with yoga, creating psychophysical exercises for actors (Hulton and Kapsali 2017). Psychophysical is a term Stanislavsky used early in his work[5] to highlight a significant problem of the western actor – the split Cartesian duality of a separate mind (psycho) and body (physical), i.e., the psycho physical. The psychophysical represents, then, an integrated body and mind.

In contrast to the psychophysical, I frame as sociopsychophysical, Kathakali's actor training processes. In Kathakali, the *guru* and *shishya* both work with their integrated body/minds, their psychophysicality. The social element in my original construct sociopsychophysical is defined by the social relationship between the teacher and learner best realised within the one-on-one actor training space. The significant trilogy of terms then adds up to the psycho physical, the psychophysical and the sociopsychophysical. Departing from an interest in the individual and

4 As Zarrilli documents, "Stanislavsky, Michael Chekhov, Meyerhold, Artaud, Brecht, Grotowski, Barba, Copeau, Tadeusz Kantor, Herbert Blau, Suzuki Tadashi, Ypshi Oida, Ariane Mnouchkine and Anne Bogart have been influenced in some way by non-Western traditions ranging from Japanese noh, Indian yoga or kathakali dance-drama, to Beijing opera, among others" (2009:8).

5 This book references Stanislavski's early work with text-based realism as here is where he had the strongest impact on 20th-century actor training in the west. His later writings on his work with actors, much of it translated and disseminated long after his death, and particularly his method of physical actions, brings western actor preparation into greater alignment with Kathakali actor training.

psychophysical, the sociopsychophysical works with the "joint action" (Sebanz, Bekkering and Knoblich 2006:70) of master and pupil.

To further elucidate the idea of the "social" I differentiate the "old social" as one that frames Kathakali's social world in India/Kerala (Gough and Schneider 1961), as specific to Kathakali texts created in the seventeenth century. This includes both the time-tested culture and practices of the traditional Kathakali acting pedagogy that have survived to this day, including the *guru shishya parampara* or the master disciple tradition. The old social frames the social weave that informs Kathakali's text and stories created in the seventeenth century, a social weave informed by the Indian caste system (Dumont 1970; Das 1977; Guha 2013). While acknowledging the tumultuous change in its social world especially since Indian Independence from colonial rule in 1947, the framing of the old social works to stay bounded within the context of seventeenth-century Kathakali texts and their social world, and not reflect more generally on Kathakali over the centuries, or on the social life of the state of Kerala. Further, the old social references culture and practices embedded within the body of the practitioner researcher. Within this practitioner-led work this Indian social weave is in part embedded into the body of the master practitioner/author and, as the body is carried from the old social in India where the practitioner lived most of his life to his new life in the new social in Australia, this distinction between the old and new social has specific meaning for the practice and its relocation. The book also assumes no hierarchical bias or prejudice between the "old" and the "new."

In contrast to the old social, the new social references the teaching of Kathakali to contemporary Australian performers in Melbourne, Australia, where I now live. This includes my new social existence as a new migrant to Australia having migrated in the year 2010, an awareness of the new social equations on offer in the multicultural Australia of 2014–18 (Hage 2002), and, with a rise of the Asian powers like China and India, the emergence of a new international order within the wider shifting realities of a globalised world. For this book, the new social is the site, then, for new negotiations within the intercultural actor-training space. This book works to contribute to the new body of knowledge that is emerging from an acknowledgement of the presence of, and the value of Asian arts to contemporary performing training in Australia.

Kathakali in context

Kathakali is a late sixteenth-century/early seventeenth-century dance theatre, created and practised primarily in the southern Indian state of Kerala. Kathakali, or story-dance, has the dancer-actor perform archetypal characters from stories such as those of the Indian epic *The Mahabharata*. Episodes from those stories were first turned into Kathakali *attakathas* or texts written for performance. These *attakathas* would be handed over by the writer to the *guru* or teacher. The *guru* then created a performance score, practising and performing each role, often for an illiterate learner. The learner would receive the instructions orally and learn his part by imitating the teacher's demonstration. Once the roles had been learnt, the performers would come together to work more formally in rehearsal with the musicians.

In rehearsal, two singers, accompanied by two percussionists, a *chenda* and a *maddalam* player, narrate the story *shlokas/dandakas* and then sing the dialogues or *padams*. Appropriate *ragas* or specific melody scores are selected to support the *bhava* or the embodied emotional state appropriate to each dialogue or *padam*. The dancer-actors enact these *padams* using hand gestures or *hasta mudras*. The stage action crafted includes the *padams* as well as *attams* or danced enactments without song and *kalashams* or pure dance pieces.

Kathakali is an eastern theatre about gods and demons, and epic human heroes and villains. *The Mahabharata*, the literary epic that inspires a large number of Kathakali stories, while existing as a literary text, has a sacred status in Indian culture. Kathakali is a religious theatre in so far as it performs stories of the epic, and is performed by, and within, a culture of a people who have religion wrapped up in large parts of their life. Kathakali evolved out of earlier forms of what were more directly religion-linked forms of performance, including *krishnaattam*, the stories of the god Krishna, and *ramanattam*, and the stories of Rama, the hero of the Ramayana, considered a sacred text by the Hindus in India. Kathakali's creator, Kottayyam Thamburan, a local royal or *thamburan* of the principality of Kottayyam in Kerala, sometime in the late seventeenth century, used the less sacred and more literary *Mahabharata* to source stories for his first set of four Kathakali plays. To perform these plays, he trained his soldiers as performers, turning them into dancing warriors. These soldiers belonged to the *nair* or *nayar* caste, reflecting the deeper entrenchment of the art form within the Indian caste system.

In Kerala, each caste, tribe or community has its own form of performance. These forms cross-influence others to create new forms. Performance sources of Kathakali include the ritualistic, classical, tribal and folk forms of Kerala, namely *theyyam, kutiyattam, kalaripayattu, krishnattam* and *ramanattam*. *Theyyam* is a ritualistic performance in which the lower-caste or untouchable performer during the course of an annually held performance becomes the temple deity, bringing alive the deity, representing the deity for the worshippers. *Kutiyattam* is a form of stylised Sanskrit drama that is performed by upper-caste temple servants called *chakyaars*. *Kalaripayattu* is a martial art performed by the warrior *nair* caste. Kathakali's pre-expressive body-training routine is directly inspired by *Kalaripayattu*. *Krishnattam* and *Ramanattam* are dance dramas created around the life stories of the two Hindu gods Krishna and Rama.

This hybridity of influence suggests a spirit of inclusiveness that exists within the Kathakali tradition. As compared to certain traditions that are closed to outsiders, within the context of actor training, this inclusiveness is reflected in contemporary Kathakali's openness to students of all castes as well as what are referred to within the Kathakali community in India as "foreign students" who are welcomed in and taught with enthusiasm. At the same time, Kathakali has an international presence with Kathakali troupes travelling the world to perform in dance and theatre festivals, university drama departments and international cultural events. Kathakali has also been engaged by practitioners like Grotowski, Barba and Mnouchkine to influence the style and craft of their actors.

Over the centuries, especially in its latest period of reinvigoration in the 1930s and 1940s, in its performance mode Kathakali has evolved by including an ever-widening body of stories and literature. In addition to a host of traditional chore-ographies and stories, these include dance dramas on Mary Magdalen, the Persian story of Sohrab and Rustum, as well as works of William Shakespeare, notably *King Lear* and *Othello*. On the other hand, any perceived conservatism as reflected through its *guru shishya* tradition and imitative pedagogy, as observed at the International Centre for Kathakali, New Delhi, is a reflection of its self-assurance, of knowing through time-tested methods what works to create Kathakali actors. Its relatively steady through line within actor training is evidenced through very similar codifications available in both Zarrilli (1984) and Balakrishnan (2005). This core stability is to be seen as a strength, and not as a consequence of any rigidity or resistance to change. Here too as the student actor matures he is encour-aged to explore an ever-growing repertoire of Kathakali dramas. Recognising limitations within western actor training, in terms of time available and knowl-edge of Kathakali's language, culture and texts, this book limits its explorations to the initial years of Kathakali training practice when the imitative pedagogy is primarily at play. It does not seek to engage western Australian actor training at advanced levels of Kathakali actor training wherein Kathakali student actors in their sixth to eight years are challenged through their imaginative faculties and textual interpretive abilities.

A "practitioner researcher"

I am a Kashmiri Brahmin. I was born in New Delhi, India. I am not a traditional Kathakali dancer from the southern Indian state of Kerala. In addition to my work as a Kathakali performer/teacher, I am also a writer and performer of my own contemporary work. I began my Kathakali training at the age of 24 after my train-ing as a contemporary actor at the London Academy of Music and Dramatic Art, U.K. Today, at 53, besides being a Kathakali master practitioner, I am also a crea-tor of contemporary performances that have succeeded locally, as well as toured the international theatre festival world. My work with Kathakali and Shakespeare has received both critical and public attention.

I began learning Kathakali from Sadanam Balakrishnan for ten years at the International Centre for Kathakali, New Delhi, where he was both principal dancer and teacher. Sadanam Balakrishnan is today a leading practitioner of Kathakali. His publi-cation, *Kathakali: A Practitioner's Perspective* (2005) is one of the relevant Kathakali texts for this book. I have also learnt Kathakali over the past years with a number of other teachers, including Evoor Rajendran Pillai, Kudamanoor Karunakaran Nair, Sadanam Naripetta, Kalamandalam Krishna Kumar and Kalamandalam Bhagyanathan. A large part of these lessons were conducted one-on-one.

My training has included numerous *uzhichill* or body massage sessions, and learning the entire *kalaripayattu*-inspired body exercise routine *meyyarappu*. My decades-long engagement includes learning and practising the entire performance score of what are considered amongst the Kathakali performer community, and acknowledged by academics, as the golden classics of Kathakali. These four plays were written and choreographed by the creator of Kathakali, Kottayyam Thamburan, in the seventeenth century. They are *Kalyana Saugandhikam* translated as the "Flower of Good Fortune," *Baka Vadhaam* or the "Death of the Monster Baka," *Kirmira Vadham* or the "Death of the Monster Kirmira" and *Kalekeya Vadham* or the "Death of the Monster Kalakeya." At the International Centre for Kathakali, New Delhi, acting and dance choreographies used for actor training are primarily from these four dance dramas which continue to influence the core practices of the Kathakali actor-training tradition. At this central location of the ethnographic research for this book each new season begins with the professional troupe revisiting, one by one, each of these four plays. To make clear, training is not restricted to these dramas, it is only that these dramas occupy a central space in the training and performance repertoire. As there is no overarching authority censoring and controlling, each institution/*guru* is also free to evolve its/his own curriculum, especially at advanced stages of learning.

The research field: methodologies, tools and paradigms

Through the teaching of contemporary performers in Australia, this book seeks to uncover original insights and knowledge that help in theorising and engaging with academics and practitioners, both in Australia and worldwide. While Kathakali is a theatre of gods and demons, and kings and queens, it is to the very human craft of actor training that this book attends. Towards this end, this project is situated within the academic discipline of "embodiment," making the living human body, with its subjective experiences and its objective social/cultural expression, the primary tool for enquiry. As Thomas Csordas (1990:94) theorises, the living body exists pre-objectively, before it is objectified by the mind as a thing, or can be discussed in terms of categories of the scientific body, for example, of body parts and fluids. It is this pre-objective, lived, subjective and felt experience that grounds, provokes and leads my enquiry. By my embodied presence in, and experience of Kathakali actor training, my body, self and culture are all provocations for knowledge gathering. The existential relationship formed with other bodies, with each individual learner, becomes fertile ground for enquiry. Out of the forging of these relationships the research forages and "knowledge gathers" foundational insights for intercultural actor training.

While the primary site of teaching Kathakali is firmly located in Melbourne, Australia, some elements of the work, i.e., the author traveling to India to gather data at the International Centre for Kathakali, New Delhi, may be seen as autoethnographic. This Kathakali training centre is where for ten years I learnt Kathakali from 1990 to 2000. The centre continues to teach the exact form and *sampradayam*[6] or tradition of Kathakali that I learnt there.

---

6 The three traditional styles of Kathakali are *Vettathu Sampradayam, Kalladikkodan Sampradyam* and *Kaplingadu Sampradayam*. These styles may further be narrowed down to the "northern" and "southern" styles. Differences in technique and choreographic choices, for example, mark a separation. The International Centre for Kathakali follows the northern style.

Methodology

To gather original and freshly minted data for this project it was important to expose Kathakali actor-training practices to a range of new learners, from different ethnic backgrounds as well as from a variety of performance practices. All the students/learners selected and participating in the intercultural knowledge-gathering exercise were doing so for the first time – they were not my existing Kathakali students.

To create the appropriate site I hired a rehearsal space in the city and through social media connected with the Melbourne performing arts community. I offered an introductory Kathakali workshop teaching Kathakali body-training practices, dance choreography and *rasaabhinaya* or the art of enacting embodied emotions. A total of 16 participants attended these workshops. These performing artists were from a range of practices, including Butoh, BodyWeather, ballet, contemporary dance, performance art, Odissi dance and stage and TV/cinema acting. There were also a few casual amateur walk-ins. My offer was to enhance their own practice by working on traditional Kathakali techniques and training practices. We worked one and a half hours a week for three months in a small, hired working space in Melbourne. Five out of the sixteen participants continued to work with me after these workshops, engaging with Kathakali actor training for their individual needs, though only three of them carried on with one-on-one work. Of these three, one of them was an Odissi dancer, trained in Indian classical dance. Though a great support through the work, she offered a limited contribution to the research exercise, as she had already journeyed to the places to which I was working to take the others. An example is the learning of two-handed hand gestures or *mudras*, which she achieved very easily, while the rest struggled to perform them, making their struggle of interest to me. This left two participants who went on to work one-on-one with me.

The two performing artists who went on to work with me from August 2014 through to June 2016, a period of 22 months, were both senior Melbourne-based performers. They both had previous experience of working with Asian forms. They had recently finished Master's degrees in practice-led research. Helen Smith is an Englishwoman, who migrated to Australia in 2008. She had done extensive work in Butoh, working with masters in Japan. She had also created original body-based performance work on the Melbourne stage. She is a tall, well-built, strong woman. In the initial workshops, she displayed a strong sense of body control and rhythm. She was able to work very hard (Figure 1.3).

The other participant was Peter Fraser, an Australian performer in his 60s who, despite his age, showed enormous physical strength and agility. Peter was both a BodyWeather practitioner and a creator of contemporary performance art. While Peter was shy and less aggressive with his body, he showed exceptional ability in all exercises that demanded body transformation. For example, in the workshops, he visibly transformed into a Kathakali vulture, elephant, deer and fish. Peter's recent work was a performance art piece undertaken for his Master's thesis. He had played a lizard living inside a glass cage. With Peter and Helen, I felt I had ideal candidates for one-on-one Kathakali training.

Figure 1.3 Helen Smith. (Photo courtesy of Darren Gill.)

Peter and Helen had never seen Kathakali, so I organised a performance of Kathakali in my home in Gisborne. Over the next three months, the three of us worked together in Helen's home in Melbourne. We then performed together in another home concert. They were part of my Kathakali lecture demonstration, working to show their newly learnt skills of Kathakali hand gestures, basic foot-work, nine emotions and some elementary Kathakali dancing.

As the work progressed and their involvement deepened, in letter and spirit, they both consented to my using the knowledge and data gathered from our work-ing relationship, including the proposed extended socialisation and deeper per-sonal engagement. I offered to teach them one-on-one. While Peter was keen, Helen was initially hesitant. She preferred working in a threesome. I thought that Peter was suffering in the group sessions, as he was slower in learning, Helen dominated the space; she was also competitive, albeit in a joyous way. She was overshadowing Peter. She also needed to slow down, observe more and interpret less. I needed to have greater control over the work with her. By presenting these arguments and explaining the framework of my creative objective, I was able to persuade them to work one-on-one.

They started coming to my home in Gisborne, in rural Victoria, an hour away from Melbourne. We had begun to form an important element of the traditional relationship, where the student travels to the teacher to gain knowl-edge. I cooked lunch for them. They met my wife Monica. We socialised together. Drank cups of tea. Chatted. We rested together in the afternoon, sometimes falling off to sleep. After working for six months, I decided they needed a greater challenge. I facilitated their travel to India to work with Evoor Rajendran Pillai, the Principal of the International Centre of Kathakali, New Delhi. They worked in India for ten days. They videotaped the Kathakali *guru*'s teaching. They lived in my home. They met and bonded with my 87-year-old father and 80-year-old mother. They shared in the social life of the house, meeting visitors, friends.

On their return to Australia, they continued to work one-on-one with me. After another six months, we created a performance at a formal theatre in Melbourne. I video-documented parts of their performance I thought relevant. After working with them for 18 months, I set up a series of interviews with Helen and Peter. I asked a Melbourne-based academic, Dr. Priya Srinivasan (2011), to facilitate these conversations, as I feared I had been their Kathakali teacher for far too long, and that this identity could continue to dominate the interview.

In addition to my work with Helen and Peter in Australia, I travelled to India and observed classes, conducted interviews and held detailed discussions with Kathakali masters at the International Centre for Kathakali, including my prime source and teacher, Evoor Rajendran Pillai. These interviews were conducted in English, Hindi and Malayalam.

Through the entire period of the work in Melbourne and fieldwork in India, I kept a diary into which were noted all observations and reflections. This process of keeping a written record facilitated what formed into a convention, one used throughout the book, of inserting reconstructions, elaborations on and actual writings from my diary, and field notes from the workshops. They are a key element of the research and are set out in what I frame as a "diary documentary" form of writing. I work with this convention whenever I need to step away from the theoretical, analytical and the literary, and give the reader a more direct reportage on the visceral embodied elements of the practice-led exercise. As the living body, the primary tool of research enquiry, exists in the present, this convention works to bring the reader into the present moment of the practice-led work.

Throughout my work with Helen and Peter, I worked with the traditional Kathakali teaching/learning methodology where the teacher demonstrates an action and the learner observes and performs the teacher's demonstrated action, and this with minimum interruption. I kept to the traditional method of not entering into a lengthy discussion, not taking notes myself in the workshop and not turning the Kathakali learner into an object of my gaze/enquiry, while continuing to encourage the concentrated, careful and sustained observation of the actions demonstrated by me. Within this teaching methodology, the only thing I was willing to do was to demonstrate the action to be performed as often as the learner asked for it. Later, I would put on the researcher's hat and reflect on the process. These reflections I recorded in my diary. This methodology maintained the authenticity of a pedagogy that has existed for centuries within a non-literate and oral tradition; the traditional learner was not literate.

Overview of chapter content

I begin the second chapter of the book introducing the reader to the traditional *guru shishya parampara* or the master–disciple relationship and its mirroring methodology. I do this through reflecting on my own one-on-one Kathakali actor-training session with Kathakali master practitioner Evoor Rajendran Pillai, Principal of the Kathakali International Centre, New Delhi. As a mature performer, I was revisiting traditional Kathakali actor-training routines previously worked with our common[7] teacher *guru* Sadanam Balakrishnan. In addition to my own subjective experience, by observing Pillai teach Gokul, one of his star pupils, an objective analysis of the *guru shishya* working relationship is presented. These two bodies are in a long-term social relationship, which is initiated each learning session through the ritualistic social practice of the learner touching the *guru*'s feet. Theorising around this old social practice, a case is made for its reconciliation within the new social, i.e., in Australia.

In Chapter 3, in response to a prejudiced and exotic perception of Kathakali as revealed in the introductory workshops in Melbourne, the real and sustained scholarship of the most prolific western academic working on Kathakali, Phillip Zarrilli, is examined. A critique of his scholarship sets up a contrast between the western practitioner's (including Zarrilli's own) Cartesian mind–body psycho physical spilt, and the eastern master practitioner's integrated sociopsychophysicality. A case is made for the master's well-functioning integrated mind/body to be placed centrally in an intercultural exercise. To locate and understand the functioning of this body of the Kathakali *guru* working with other bodies of other cultures, the intercultural work of seminal European theatre anthropologist Eugenio Barba is read into by examining the literature around Barba's extensive work at the Odin Teatret, specifically highlighting certain moments of intercultural conflict between him and one of the founding members of the Odin Teatret, the Indian Odissi dance *guru* Sanjukta Panigrahi. These incidents centre on the ritual of feet touching. These sites of conflict between Panigrahi and Barba centred on these incidents of feet touching are used to search for a theoretical framework, and an understanding of the specific social weave of the old social, a social weave that, it is argued, is informed by the Indian caste system. Values embedded within the caste system need to be paid attention to and re-valued, in the intercultural context of teaching an Indian art form in Australia.

Chapter 4 sets out the teaching of Kathakali to contemporary performers in Australia in the group workshop mode. In negotiating the problems and difficulties faced in teaching a group of learners, creative solutions on offer are recorded, even while recognising that this process of creative problem-solving takes the teaching work away from the traditional mirroring methodology. Referencing the experiences of the group exercise Chapter 5 explores more rigorously the traditional *guru shishya* methodology through the one-on-one site.

---

7 While Balakrishnan is not Pillai's *guru*, he was the Principal of the Center and Pillai a senior performer in the professional company working under his direction. I make this clarification as lineage is important in Kathakali and performers are sensitive to any misrepresentation.

In Chapter 5, the training of two Australian performers, Helen Smith and Peter Fraser, is examined, and the work done towards validating the one-on-one site for Kathakali actor training is documented. In teaching Helen and Peter one-on-one, the author/researcher was looking to find ways and means to persuade them to follow his primary objective, an appreciation of the mirroring methodology. While recording the difficulties faced in this process, the chapter addresses a key question of the existence of the performer's aesthetic pleasure or *rasa*. Do performers experience *rasa*? In this chapter, work is done to share the practice-led work as well as theories around the question of the performer's pleasure or *rasa*.

Chapter 6 negotiates the social phenomenon of caste and how it reflects in/ within Kathakali texts and performativity. As Kathakali texts were written for, and first performed by *nair* warrior/soldiers a collective framing of aggressive martial gestures may be referred to as "Kathakali's gestures of embodied aggression." These outwardly directed sociopsychophysical gestures are performed to complex Kathakali rhythms or *taalams* and are a prime offering to the psychophysically absorbed and introverted western performer. This chapter examines the complexity of the Indian caste system and seeks to understand its meaning and effect within Kathakali texts and performativity.

Acknowledging the challenges faced of translating the text and practices of a seventeenth-century Indian dance drama to contemporary actors/performers in Australia, the seventh chapter documents the adaptations made to the traditional teaching curriculum. While exploring the traditional texts and practices, the author works further to individualise the performances of Helen and Peter performing Kathakali in Australia. The individualised performances were worked through using the vehicle of the author's production of *The Magic Hour*, in which scenes of Shakespeare's *Othello* have been adapted to the Kathakali form. An analysis follows, of Helen and Peter's "innercultural" performances of Kathakali and Shakespeare, as well as a documentation made of what this book presents as Kathakali's prime offering to the western performer, i.e., an experience of *rasa* through performing its gestures of embodied aggression.

The final chapter works to widen the scope beyond the Australian experience, making the knowledge, practices and claims realised relevant for the twenty-first-century global actor/performer. While appreciating Camelli's "post psychophysical" interrelationship between the performer's body/mind and the "sociomaterial" conditions of the performance, including a relationship with technology, the special creative human bond between two bodies/minds in the *guru shishya* sociopsychophysical tradition is reiterated. The success of the practice-led one-on-one work in Australia opens up the possibility globally of one-on-one actor training being explored more rigorously in contemporary intercultural actor-training programs. While the workshop mode of actor training is common practice and will continue to be the norm, an addition to each workshop of the one-on-one mode, it is suggested, will further deepen the work of the teacher, master practitioner or workshop conductor.

2 The *guru shishya* or master disciple relationship

I begin this journey of sharing with the reader my teaching of Kathakali to performers in Australia by first reflecting on the traditional Indian *guru shishya parampara* or master disciple relationship. I do it through a documentation and analysis of my own one-on-one Kathakali actor-training session with my teacher and Kathakali master practitioner Evoor Rajendran Pillai as well as of him training one of his star pupils Gokul at the International Centre for Kathakali, New Delhi, India. Besides further honing my own teaching skills for the work ahead of training performers in Australia, the objective in these one-on-one actor-training sessions was to reflect more deeply on the nature of Kathakali's imitative methodology. Over the two decades of learning Kathakali, I have never felt I was mimicking my teachers. By working through insights gained through the latest research in neuroscience, the act of mimicry is reframed as a mirroring; my body mirrors my teacher's body. From this shift comes the central theme of this book, an encouragement for the Australian performer to mirror the Kathakali master.

The imitative methodology of the *guru shishya* tradition

In 1987, as a 24-year-old actor training at the London Academy of Music and Dramatic Art (U.K.), I had the opportunity to participate in a workshop conducted by Ariane Mnouchkine at the Théâtre du Soleil, Paris. During the audition/interview conducted by Mnouchkine, she suggested I stop wasting my time in Europe, and return to India, and learn Kathakali with Mr. Balakrishnan, who had worked with her actors. As it happened, I followed her advice and I was Sadanam Balakrishnan's student for ten years from 1990 to 2000. Since then, I have continued to learn, teach and perform Kathakali. Rajendran Pillai was Sadanam Balakrishnan's senior artist in the centre's professional company and a master practitioner in his own right, and over the years I have continued to learn from him and from other *gurus*.

In all my years of learning from traditional masters I did not experience the act of imitating the master practitioner as anything other than an exciting artistic challenge. The skill of the teachers was excellent, their leadership extraordinary, their pride in their art, deep and rich. It is from this perspective that I react to what is a foundational piece of western anthropological writing by Zoete and Spies:[1]

> Dancing of whatever kind is done entirely by imitation, the pupil dancing behind an older dancer, who has become a teacher, as well as behind or in front of her *guru*. It seems almost impossible that such intricacy of dance movements and accents should ever be memorized, but it is astonishing to see with what rapidity they feel their way into the long series of complicated movements. Nothing is explained, the dance is gradually absorbed, rather as we might imagine a performing dog to receive his training, by receiving the impress of his teacher.
>
> (Zoete and Spies 1938:38)

If this were true, no contemporary performer, from any culture, would accept a dog and master relationship with a Kathakali *guru*. When I first read this I needed to breathe deeply for a while, to calm down. This is not an isolated vision, but in part sets the ground and equation, as far back as in 1938, for the west's vision and interpretation of the east's imitative pedagogy, with mimicry as the word most commonly used in a majority of western literature describing the imitative act (Zarrilli 2000a:92, 2011:249, Barba and Sazenbach 1967:38). The Oxford dictionary has mimicry down as "the action or skill of imitating someone or something, especially in order to entertain or ridicule." Throughout this book I work to offer an alternative vision. While appreciating western respect for individualism and individuality, I suggest that a renewed effort needs to be made for a deeper understanding of what may be understood as eastern cultures of dualism and duality.

Guru shishya in Kathak dance pedagogy

My concern for a more sophisticated and nuanced approach to the imitative in the *guru shishya* training pedagogy is shared by Monica Dalidowicz (2015), albeit in the field of *kathak*, a North Indian form of dance, and its teaching in North America. Kathak training, with its *guru shishya* pedagogy, is similar to Kathakali. In her article examining the creativity involved in Kathak dance training in the diaspora, she suggests:

> the guru-shishya parampara (master-disciple relationship), has historically been based on imitative and repetitive pedagogies. Yet close examination reveals less conspicuous forms of creativity at work in the process of reproducing the tradition with fidelity; this improvisational work is further heightened in the demands of teaching in the diaspora.
>
> (838)

---

1 Beryl Drusilla de Zoete was an English ballet dancer, critic and researcher. In the field of dance, she researched South Asian dance and acting traditions. With Walter Spies, she collaborated on *Dance and Drama in Bali* (1937), which is still considered a significant work used to reference traditional Balinese dance and theatrical forms.

Her need to examine and argue for a creativity involved in traditional pedagogy comes from an awareness similar to mine regarding a reductive and simplified representation of the imitative process which she suggests is made more complex by the innovation and creativity of each *guru* adapting to the needs of a fresh generation of learners. Fidelity to tradition, far from being inevitable, was an achievement that was actively worked on, slowly and meticulously crafted through years of study, in the North Indian dance of Kathak. Disciplined training was central to the recipe, but most descriptions of transmission of bodily knowledge in South Asian performance describe learning simply as a process of "observe, imitate, and repeat" (839).

Dalidowicz shares my concern regarding a more nuanced representation of the "observe, imitate, repeat" methodology. However, our answers, offered to similar questions, diverge. While she is concerned with innovation, adaptation and creativity, I am engaged more directly with the imitative process itself, a process that is central to the teaching methodology. It is, then, to the conservative act of observing, imitating and repeating that the analysis in this chapter attends to, arguing for a more complex and nuanced approach to this pedagogic methodology, especially as realised in the one-on-one actor-training space.

In the traditional system of training, a part of the learning happened as a one-on-one teacher-to-learner transfer of skill and knowledge. This intimate encounter, often in a small room within the teacher's house over months and years, sets up both the subjective and objective growth of the learner and the art. Throughout the learning process, the learner has the image of the action to be imitated both internally, as in his mind/memory from having observed performances, and externally by the teacher demonstrating the action. The learner observes and then performs this action. They mirror what they remember of the form, and then mirror the form as shown by the teacher. Over time and through a sustained intersubjectivity, the learner trades places, gaining the skills and being of the teacher and eventually becoming a teacher, while carrying on the tradition.

Richard Schechner (1985) alludes to this depth when he suggests "aesthetic acting, learned from the outside, 'composed' and culturally determined, penetrates deep into the brain. What was at the start of the training an external effect becomes during the course of training an internal cause" (273). It is this astonishing and mysterious penetration deep into the brain that this chapter works to share. A rationalisation of this transformation first exists in the length of time taken, and second, in the very social nature of this learning process. For years, the training takes place in a social setting, between the learner and the teacher and later with the singers and musicians. The first set of socialised feelings that comes into play is that of the personal feelings of a *shishya* for a *guru* and of a *guru* for a *shishya*. Right at the start, both know that this is a relationship for a considerable length of time. Consequently, it has its rules and codes of obedience and responsibility. This is the subjective condition that exists even as the objective process unravels. As much as the student is in the care of the teacher, he/she also needs to be careful of the teacher. His/her personal feelings range from love and affection for his teacher to a fear and terror of the teacher. The personal feelings of the learner are always engaged and are the subjective condition of the learning process. Often, in just a small room, the teacher demonstrates through his imposing presence and the learner mirrors what he/she observes. To understand what happens in this intimate setting, I reference my own experience of training one-on-one with master practitioner Rajendran Pillai.

The practitioner researcher in a one-on-one training session

At the International Centre for Kathakali in New Delhi, the Principal Evoor Rajendran Pillai lives in a small room on the first floor of the building that houses the centre. If he was living in a house, he would have invited me home to train one-on-one. Here at the centre, we will train in the main hall on the ground floor. This is the same space in which I will also observe him training his star student Gokul. This is also the same space that I have worked in earlier with Sadanam Balakrishnan. It has years of memories associated with it. In this space, the professional company practices with the musicians. Once a month, a Kathakali performance is held here. On weekends, students practice here in large groups formed according to the level of training achieved. On social occasions such as the festival of *Onam*, the larger community gathers in this hall to sit down and eat a meal together. It was then a very social space in which our session was being held.

The following observations are drawn from my diary at the time I commenced my work with Pillai on 16 July 2016. This forms the "diary documentary" convention used throughout this book.

It is for the first time that I am entering Kathakali training space with a video camera in hand. I feel very uncomfortable about this and it makes me feel like a tourist coming to take photographs of exotic Kathakali dancing. I have to persuade myself that this documentation is an important element of the research for this book, especially as I will be at the centre of it, as a performer/learner and teacher. The room has changed. They have put in air conditioners to beat the Delhi heat, but this means all the windows are shut. As I am unsure of the protocol to switch on air conditioners, I suspect they are there for performances held over the weekend, I locate the fan switches and switch on the fans. The air is hot and muggy with an expectancy of the monsoon rain. I set up Pillai's stool to sit on and wait for his arrival. I can hear him outside talking on his cell phone. Perhaps to his wife in Kerala? His son is also named Arjun. His daughter is Rajashri. I stand waiting in the middle of the room wearing my north Indian attire of a *kurta* and *pyjama*, feeling a little apprehensive about the session. I wonder how intense he will make the session for me? How hard he will make me work? At 52, I have my niggling aches and pains and worries. But I am also excited. I have stood here waiting for the teacher to arrive, many times over, over the many years.

Pillai, who I will now refer to as I call him, Rajendran ji, steps into the hall and immediately indicates for me to do the formal greeting salutation. While I do the formal salutation, I see he does not sit down on the stool but stands and waits for me to finish. As Rajendran ji and I are almost the same age (he is a few years older than me), at the moment I reach out to touch his feet he holds my arms and prevents me from bending. A gentle bowing of the head with folded hands is enough of an expression of respect. He too responds with a nod and a folded hand greeting. We are then both ready to begin the session.

I had earlier shared with him my objective of doing one-on-one training, which includes my going back to Australia and teaching Kathakali one-on-one, and he, I think, has come in with a plan that I suspect involves him demonstrating to me all the exercises for a model session, as well as correcting my Kathakali form. Not surprisingly, immediately after the salutation, he steps up beside me, takes three quick steps backwards and then moves into what I know as the basic Kathakali posture. The salutation has now become a little danced step and choreography. He tells me to observe, and then performs the salutation, followed by the three danced steps, and then moves his body into the basic posture. He suggests this sequence is the first thing I do with a learner. He expects me to do it perfectly and even though I have done both the salutation and the basic posture many times over the years, the sequence proves a challenge. *Tala* or rhythm is my weakest ability and even this minimal choreography sets up a challenge. I seem to be imitating him with less grace and rhythm. He decides to lead the way by chanting the rhythm even as he does the actions. The rhythm is *chembata* and the *vaitari* or the spoken sound pattern *ti ti tai*. With great ease, he demonstrates and locates every action of the choreography within this rhythm. The salutation, the three steps backwards and the arrival into the basic step are all performed to the rhythm of *ti ti tai* and *ti ti tai*. Even in this little bit of body movement, while I imitate some aspects of his body form, I have to find a deeper place within myself, to sense his ease with the rhythm, with the body moving to *tala*. I have to watch him more carefully sensing how his body relaxes into the rhythm, allowing the rhythm to lead. I also sense the continuity of movement, the flow through the entire action. He encourages me to speak the rhythm and when I do I find I have to first get the same flow in the spoken sounds and then allow them to lead the movement. My body begins to work with itself, with its own spoken rhythm as I seem to commune with myself. He demonstrates the action a few times, then stands aside beating the rhythm with his hands and chanting the rhythm. I hold my own spoken rhythm in my head and then listen to his chant and follow with my body. After a few attempts we both laugh, delighting at getting this elementary action right. He then indicates that I stay in the basic posture, expecting me to hold it for a while. I know, after a minute or two of holding the basic posture, the pain in the thigh muscles starts kicking in and this exercise gets harder to hold. However, today, Rajendra ji has decided I need to go lower, deeper into the posture, and he keeps indicating with his right hand, asking me to go lower and stay down. While I hold the posture, he walks up to me, makes me stretch my knees wider, places his hands on my lower back suggesting I curve the back in a little more, and then he moves to my hands, asking me to relax my wrists, and release my hands. I have done this basic posture an endless number of times over the years, and yet each time, there is a new alignment, a new adjustment, a new way the body seems to form itself into the basic pose.

Now seeing the work through the eyes of a scholar writing self-consciously about the craft of Kathakali, I realise the potential for embodied knowledge of this one embodied action. I will describe it here in greater detail. In this next section, I theorise an understanding and an experience of the basic posture, referencing ideas received from Drew Leder in his seminal work, *The Absent Body* (1990).

The basic posture

An appreciation of crafting a performer's body into the Kathakali form is facilitated through an understanding of the phenomenology of Drew Leder's "disappearing body" (1990:1). The phenomenology of the body and its disappearance has been the subject of his detailed inquiry in *The Absent Body*:

> While in one sense the body is the most abiding and inescapable presence in our lives, it is also essentially characterized by absence. That is, one's own body is rarely the thematic object of experience. When reading a book or lost in thought, my own bodily state may be the farthest thing from my awareness. I experientially dwell in a world of ideas, paying little heed to my physical sensations or postures.
>
> (1)

The idea of the disappearing body came from what Leder described as the phenomenology of the body's disappearance "even in the midst of its inescapable presence" (1).

By the body's disappearance Leder implied that, as the senses experience the world, the sense organs themselves recede and disappear into the background. As an example, he suggests that you are least aware of your eye at the point that your eye observes the horizon. Or an apple, once eaten, leaves no trace of its previous taste, touch, smell or sight. With it being physically consumed into the body, its sensory experience too is consumed by each organ. These sense organs, including the human skin that covers the entire body, Leder calls the "surface body" (1). This surface body he suggests is in a constant "ecstatic" or outward engagement with the world.

As leading western academic writing on Kathakali Phillip Zarrilli suggests, "Physiologically, the surface body is characterized primarily by exteroception" (2004:658), implying that the outer-directed five senses open us out to the external world. For Leder this "exteroception" of the surface body can be "without immediate emotional response" (40). The exteroception of the surface body does not by itself generate an emotional response. For there to be an emotional response in the body, the surface body must actively reach out, or engage with the world. Seeing a flower in itself does not create an emotion of joy within. To experience an emotion of joy the surface body needs to actively engage with and needs to move towards the flower: to smell it deeper, to see it clearer, to touch it. In so doing, by its active exteroception, the body recedes into the background or disappears.

Simultaneous to the phenomenology of the disappearing body is the phenomenology of its continued centrality. Wherever our body moves to, it continues to be at the centre of its experience, whether sitting, standing or running. Whether on top of a mountain, by a river or by the ocean. The body is always present, defining the here, to the world out there. By this, as the surface body opens itself out to the world, the body is continuously in a state of disappearance. Thus, continually, the surface body, by its very ecstatic or outward stance, leads to the body's recession or disappearance from experience. Citing Leder, Zarrilli (2004:660) suggests that the body's disappearance and absence thereby mark our "ceaseless relation to the world" (Leder 1990:160). The problem that our ceaseless relation to the world and phenomenology of the surface body and the consequent disappearing body creates for the Kathakali learner is a sense of disembodiment, and an instability between the *angik* (objective physical body) and the *stavik* (subjective emotional state). Not sure of his/her own body and its stable embodied presence, the learner struggles to create and sustain an embodied presence. Kathakali solves this problem with its intensive embodied stabilisation and integration of the subjective and objective or the emotional and physical. The Kathakali form is crafted to hold within itself, as it were, at every moment, both the physical *angika* or embodied and the *bhava* or emotional state. The first step, then, in the long and arduous process of Kathakali performer training is the crafting of the performer's body into a basic posture.

Presence and Kathakali training: the basic posture

In the basic Kathakali posture, the feet are placed in parallel, slightly wider than shoulder-width apart, with the head and trunk aligned right in the middle, with the trunk lowered, the knees bent outward and with the weight resting on the outer edges of both feet. The toes curl inward in an arc with the big toe pressing down hardest while clamping the foot to the ground. The lower back is then pressed inwards towards the belly, and both arms rest stretched wide to each side. The breathing through this process is relaxed, slow and deep. The body is continuously lowered and kept down.

This posture, with its low centre of gravity, allows the heavy costume to be carried with ease. The costume includes a set of heavy jewellery carved out of wood and layers of starched cloth supporting the billowing skirt, whose weight and sway demand the technique of holding the feet outward with the weight on the outer edge; if the feet were placed flat on the ground, the knees would collapse inward. The wearing of the large Kathakali headdress, the *kiridam*, creates a further imbalance, shaped as it is with its back portion flat and its front curving out in a concave shape, making it front heavy. The control of the lower back then allows the upper body to be tilted backwards at a right angle so as to balance the headdress, perfectly countering the forward bias. The *kiridam* plays an important role, with the head staying balanced and stable with its shape and weight. This prevents the performer from figuratively losing his head when the emotional intensity of the scene increases, and the drumming starts going wild. The headdress must remain stable through all the rage expressed.

These coordinated adjustments of various muscles of the body allow for an "extra daily" ability to both balance a heavy costume and headdress and dance, emote and enact powerfully. Illustrating one of theatre anthropologist Eugenio Barba's "recurring principles"[2] is the continuous ritualised game of "balance in action" that Kathakali choreography embodies. This extra daily ability to balance and unbalance while wearing the heavy costume and headdress, whether it be moving forwards or backwards, tilting to the right or left, or dancing around in a circle, emerges from and is an elaboration of the daily, unconscious game of balance and unbalance, the daily business of keeping our feet on the ground and our lives steady. This extra daily ability to balance in action helps stabilise the earlier mentioned problem of the performer's disembodied sense of instability, of the imbalanced inner and outer, of an embodied ecstasy and recession, and gives the performer a sense of a stable embodied self, an embodied self in control.

Central to this business of balance in action is the lowering of the performer's body. The entire training of the Kathakali performer involves the steady lowering of the centre of gravity and the shifting of weight from one foot to the other. The lower the centre of gravity and the deeper the weight rests on each clamping foot, the easier it is to balance the headdress. The low centre of gravity further helps in the extra daily transfer of weight from one foot to the other. Through shifts in tempo-rhythm, these weighed-down danced steps help in the generation, stability and control of the *bhava* or the embodied emotional state. For example, as the character gets angrier, the tempo-rhythm builds up; when speeding up, the performer must stay down, keeping his centre of gravity low. Even as the force, energy and weight are sent downward into the earth, the *bhava* or the emotional state is generated through the body to be expressed formally through the appropriate facial gesture.

A common misrepresentation of Kathakali aesthetics has *bhava* existing only on/in the face, through facial gestures. In Kathakali (as in other Indian dance traditions like *odissi* and *bharatanatyam*), the entire body is trained to embody the emotional state. The dancer's body is perceived to have *bhava*. The balanced head and the *kiridam* keep in control the enormously powerful extra daily energy generated in the dancer's body. The skilled performer learns to use the power in his feet to generate, as if from the earth, the required energy to embody and sustain the *bhava*. This then is Kathakali's craft of a balance in action that creates an extra daily ability to balance and create powerful embodied emotional states of being which are best described as a Kathakali performer's "presence."

2 Barba's "recurring principles" or "shared themes of performativity" between a number of eastern and western performance traditions, which include oppositional binaries such as "altered balance, dynamic opposition, consistent in-consistency, reduction, and equivalence" (1995:9).

Absence and Kathakali training

This extra daily presence brings us to examine its reflexive other, a subjective state of "absence." This state of absence by its primary condition of disappearance is thematically difficult to describe and detail. This condition of absence, however, exists, is crafted and realised through a commitment to and a perfection of the Kathakali form. Even as the objective outer Kathakali form is crafted as a presence, the inner subjective state is experienced as an absence. An own-embodied experience of the subjective condition of the Kathakali form leads one away from describing the inner experience as empty or neutral. Subjectively, the performer exists as an absence, as a performed reflexive other of the embodied presence.

To understand and clarify this phenomenon, I would like to give the example of a hand with the outer surface of the hand placed against a cold wind. While the texture of the outer surface feels colder, harder and with a presence, the inner surface of the palm is calmer, softer and with a reflexive sense of the other, of an absence. The Kathakali basic posture offers the opportunity to try and detail this state of subjective absence. The basic posture demands the spreading out of the body, the stretching of the skin and a filling out of the form by the entire surface body of the performer. It is as if the skin of the performer is stretched to its limit. Even as the performer embodies the form, his own body seems to disappear. The more the performer's body embodies and becomes at ease with the form of the Kathakali basic posture, the more this sense of disappearance of his own body formalises within the performer as an inner state of absence. This absence is cultivated into a subjective habit. A good teacher repeats the basic posture often while making the student hold the posture for increasing lengths of time. This is done not only to perfect the outer shape of the Kathakali form but also to cultivate the inner subjective space.

This ability to create absence seems a contradictory outcome of intense Kathakali training. From the extra daily body techniques utilised, it would make sense if, instead of an embodied absence, a stylised and extra daily presence resulted. This is true, of course; this ability is developed. However, the counter-ability is also created, exists and is present on the stage when the performer is not performing. The Kathakali performer, elaborately made up, costumed and transformed into an epic character or god is often asked, while the other performer is performing, to wait and do nothing. At these times he cannot collapse back into his daily self. Nor can he disturb the performance of the other performer with his active presence. Instead, he must wait with a formalised, calm outer presence and a calmer, inner subjective state of absence.

The basic body posture then is not just an embodied objective presence but also is an embodied subjectivity experienced within as an absence. The extra daily body techniques of Kathakali training help the performer arrive at this perfect balance. Often while working with my teacher Sadanam Balakrishnan and standing in the basic posture, he would refer to the fact that he could see, like a passing shadow, Arjun, that is me. He would then say that he did not want to see Arjun but only Kathakali. Initially bewildered, over time, I understood what he meant. I learnt to stand in the basic posture, without, even for a brief moment, my own inner presence and struggle visible. This inner presence may be understood as a set of resistances, that inner struggle with the effort and commitment towards the creation of the outer form. In time, this struggle settled. In time, all that I was, was an embodied Kathakali basic posture with a calm inner state of absence.

Mirroring the Kathakali *guru's* basic posture

Returning to the one-on-one session, Rajendran ji decides to stand facing me in the basic posture and work me through the logic of the body structure, even as he insists I do this exercise every day with new students and learners. "This is a must" he says in English, which he speaks reasonably fluently. He lowers himself into the stance, adjusts his feet a little for width, and then seems to visibly expand in front of me as he both seems to lower himself deeper towards the ground, as well as works to pull back and hold the body at the centre with his lower back, while widening his chest and expanding both his arms sideways like the branches of a tree. His arms are not straight out but slightly curved at the inner elbow. Then, once he seems to have completely settled into the form, he releases his hands from the wrist and lets them drop freely. He gently bounces his hands as if to display the ease and freedom of his hands. I notice while his feet, and especially his big toe, are gripping the ground hard, his hands are doing the opposite, they are in Rajendran ji's words "loose and free" with "no tension".

I mirror his embodiment of the basic posture, realising for the first time the tension in my wrists and my hands, not as free and easy as his. I reflect and recall my other teachers' bodies even as I watch Rajendran ji's. Each one had their own individual way of gripping the ground with their foot, of lowering the body, of widening the chest and arms and especially of releasing the hands. I notice Rajendran ji does a little adjustment to the back of his neck that allows him to find the right placing of the head on the neck. This slight adjust not only works for the head but also opens up the face so that it is neither looking downwards or upwards, but is comfortably looking ahead. Once his entire body is in place, he gently brings a smile to his lips, suggesting he is completely in control. I mirror his body and sense/commune with my own even as I work to understand the offerings of this seminal moment.

While mirroring the basic pose objectively, from the outside, over time the learner begins to own it from the inside, with the basic pose informed by the individual's inner commitment. This basic pose is the scaffolding readied to receive the full weight of the archetype, both in terms of the heavyweight of the costume and headdress, and in terms of the subjective passions of the epic character or god. The exercise of the basic pose sits centrally at the heart of Kathakali training.

Kannusadhakam: the eye exercise

Keeping me standing in the basic pose, though with a little less pressure of keeping low, and with my arms crossed across my chest, Rajendran ji takes me through what are singularly the most famous and exotic of Kathakali exercises, *kannusadhakam* or the eye exercise. Rajendran ji stands facing me, and directs the movements of my eyes, vertically, horizontally, diagonally and then in figures of eight, working through slow, medium and fast tempos. By the time we end, I have tears in my eyes and feel exhausted.

In comparison to this brief description of *kannusahdhakam*, I have consciously spent a lot more time earlier detailing and explaining the basic pose, which sits centrally in Kathakali actor training while the eye exercise is highlighted in most western narratives of Kathakali actor training. Eugenio Barba, the first significant European practitioner to engage with Kathakali, after his brief sojourn to India in 1963, having only observed and not performed them, documented and practised these Kathakali eye exercises as part of the Odin Teatret actor-training process. While every individual exercise is an integral part of the Kathakali form, with the basic pose working centrally to bring together all elements of the body, the sin-gling out of the eye exercise for special mention leads the exotic narrative, doing no real service to intercultural Kathakali actor training (Figure 2.1).

Figure 2.1 The powerful eyes of sage Parushuram (Kottakkal Kesavan Kundlayar). (Photo courtesy of Sreenath Narayan.)

Chuzhippu

To connect the eye movement (that expresses the emotions) with the hand gestures (that narrate the story), Rajendran ji then demonstrates the *chuzhippu*, which has the eyes following the hand gestures. There are six types of *chuzhippu*, and these are performed very slowly to facilitate the performer's concentration. The objective is to unify the hand gesture with the movement of the eye. This helps the eye be present where the physical action is, and through the eye's presence the performer's mind, emotion and being are trained to be present.

Kaal sadhakam or footwork

Having worked me hard with the basic pose and the eye exercises Rajendran ji moves me onto Kathakali *kaal sadhakam*[3] or footwork. He works at this for 30 minutes, making me repeat each step a number of times. However, he also insists I chant the *vaitari* or spoken chant that accompanies each step. This complicates the repetitive act for now, as I have to integrate my foot movement to my chant. Once again, while the process is initiated by him demonstrating the step and me observing, imitating and repeating it, the process moves very quickly to my communing with my own chant, making my feet listen to my own chant. I find sometimes my feet are leading the chant, and sometimes the chant leads my step. At the rare moments when they come together, I feel the force of the body moving powerfully to rhythm. Throughout this exercise, Rajendran ji keeps reminding me to keep the body lowered. He gets up and demonstrates the difference between doing this exercise erect or lowering the body really deep and then working the steps. The difference is enormous. With the body lowered, the entire body is committed to the act and the concentration is deeply within. If the body is held up, then the steps are much lighter, the feet seem separate from the body and the concentration moves from inside the body to the outside.

I can feel the grounding, lowering and deepening of the work strengthened by this footwork. There are four footwork routines, and in the 30 minutes we cover all four. By the end of this session, I am dripping with sweat. This is hard work.

Step One: has the footwork directed to a central point, as if drilling a hole into the earth. I call this exercise a body rooting exercise. This step is done in slow, medium and fast tempos. The *vaitari* (or vocal chant) that accompanies this step is:

Dhi ta ta ta × 4

Step Two: has the foot being slapped firmly and hard onto the earth's surface. The heel is then clicked followed by a stamping of the left and right foot. I call

---

3 For a descriptive of this particular exercise in one of Kathakali's source forms, Kutiyattam, see Madhavan, A. and Nair, S. (2013).

this exercise a body grounding exercise. This step is done in slow, medium and fast tempos. The *vaitari* (or vocal chant) that accompanies this step is:

Tai hita ti ti Tai hita tom tom × 4

In this way, each step can be seen to be serving a specific body function. The third and fourth steps, however, move away from the body stabilising imperative and are more decorative in nature. There, the energy is not directed downward and into the earth, but more along the surface and outward towards the audience. Each step has its individuality, its individual function.

For each step, Rajendran ji gets up and demonstrates. Once again, I observe carefully and then mirror his actions. I work to synchronise the chant with the step. I notice the way his right foot comes in bang on time. It's the quick lifting of the right foot that allows for a perfect timing. He demonstrates this for me at the fastest tempo, and then we both do the step together. I can sense both our bodies in communion with each other as well as with our chanting selves. We are working as much within ourselves as we are without. We are working to ground ourselves as much as we are perfecting the physicality of the step. It is this "grounding" ability, of learning to hold one's ground, that will help later when the musicians come in, and the drums start leading the performance. The performer then has literally to hold his ground, and not get swept away by the drumming.

With this work, my one-on-one session ends. It has been hard work for me as I have had to stay low and grounded for the greater part of an hour-and-a-half. Rajendran ji has also worked hard as he got up from his stool repeatedly to demonstrate a step for me, to observe and mirror. I end the session and begin to offer to bend to touch his feet, but Rajendran ji prevents me. I fold my hands in a salutation, and he too folds his hands and thanks me.

These counter gestures of my offering to touch, and his not letting me touch his feet reflect a nuanced interaction between two ageing practitioners. Rajendran ji, by not letting me bend to touch his feet, was acknowledging my age and status as a mature teacher and performer. My offer to touch was an acknowledgement of the space and culture I was in, where respect for the embodied presence of the teacher is expressed by this particular ritual. While I have personal reservations around this social practice, as shared in the later part of this chapter, there were times when I was younger, like at formal ceremonies, where everyone is touching the feet of the *guru*, that I have had to fall in line with everyone else, and touch the feet of the *guru*. But I had always felt uncomfortable about it and was happy for Rajendran ji's gesture of letting me off.

Mirroring the master: observing the master teach a star pupil

In this next section I observe and document *guru* Evoor Rajendran Pillai teaching his student Gokul, one-on-one. This objective observation of Pillai and Gokul working together is further layered by my experience of having learnt Kathakali at the same institution. Pillai was teaching Gokul the same actions I had learnt earlier from my teacher Sadanam Balakrishnan. As a consequence of my own experience, I cannot see Gokul's actions objectively, without simultaneously thinking, feeling, reflecting on the times when I performed those actions. This furthers my ability to share with the reader both the subjective and objective conditions of Kathakali actor training.

These intertwining subjective and objective perceptions of Kathakali actor training validate what for Csordas forms as a "dual locus of culture" (2008:111). Through the subjective and objective perception of the Kathakali body, I work to discover new insights into both Kathakali actor training, as well as the particular weave and culture of its social world.

Observing bodies in communion

At my request, Pillai invites me to the Kathakali Centre to watch a one-on-one session with one of his star pupils, Gokul. This is on a hot summer morning in Delhi. There are just the three of us in the session that begins at 7 a.m. and ends at 8.30 a.m., following which I have been invited to eat breakfast with Pillai in their communal kitchen. Pillai lives on the first floor. As Principal of the Kathakali Centre, as the International Centre for Kathakali is referred to by the community, he has his own small room. The other teachers stay in a large dormitory. Pillai lives on his own. His wife and two children live in Kerala as he cannot afford to have them living with him in Delhi, a far more expensive city. He sees them for a couple of months a year.

I arrive on time, having caught the newly introduced Delhi Metro rail, and having walked the short distance to the Kathakali Centre. Pillai and Gokul are both ready for me. Pillai begins the one-on-one session with Gokul, his 14-year-old male student. Gokul seems to be very happy for me to be there and observe. He smiles, beams at me. For the first 15 minutes of their hour-and-a-half-long session, Pillai takes Gokul through a series of preliminary body exercises. As Gokul knows these exercises, having worked with Pillai for a number of years, Pillai does not have to demonstrate the exercises. He stands alongside Gokul, and not facing him. This is an opportunity for the 55-year-old master practitioner to stay fit. I notice that he has a bit of a belly.

He performs each exercise energetically and Gokul immediately follows with equal vigour. As an example, Pillai jumps a kind of frog leap, known as *chattam*, 25 times. Gokul follows with another 50. He is many years younger and needs to do more than the master. In the July heat of the north Indian city of Delhi, their bodies have begun to sweat. Both are wearing white cotton *pyjamas* and are bare-bodied above the waist.

After the initial preliminary body training exercises, Pillai sits down on a stool. Gokul places a wooden block in front of him. The learning session now begins with Gokul performing the formal greeting ritual and then bending his head and reaching out to touch Pillai's feet. The teacher acknowledges the learner's body by touching his head with his right hand. He then takes the right hand and touches it to his own heart and forehead. Then he waves away the gestures, upwards, heaven words.

Having marked one end of the learning space by touching his teacher's feet, Gokul then moves to stand a short distance, three metres or so, away from the teacher. This action of touching the teacher's feet helps mark the presence of two separate bodies. The learning process may now begin within the clarity of this embodied relationship. I know the text they are working on. It is from one of the four classics of Kathakali titled *Kalayana Saugandhikam*, from here on translated as "The Flower of Good Fortune." Bhīma, one of the five *pandava* brothers, is entering a forest and frightening all the animals. Perhaps Pillai has chosen this set choreography for today's one-on-one session as he knows I am particularly interested in this play. We had discussed it extensively in an interview I had conducted with him earlier in the week.

Pillai begins the training session by beating time with a wooden stick or *taalam* on a wooden block placed in front of him. He uses his right hand to do this. He sings the text/story and gestures with his left hand, leading Gokul, who stands in front, facing him. I observe that the action of the learner is a constant to-and-fro motion, moving either towards the seated teacher or away from him. He also moves sideways, making a large square box on the ground.

As Gokul seems to know the dance well, Pillai conducts most of the session sitting. He only gets up twice to demonstrate a difficult step. Gokul observes him intently as if from deep within. The sitting down of the teacher is an important element of stabilising the relationship. It leaves the learner standing vertical, empowered and looking down at the sitting *guru*.

Now, while sitting on his stool, Pillai leads the session with his hands and with his face. With one hand he beats the rhythm to the song he sings, and with the other makes the relevant hand gestures or *mudras*. These gestures illustrate the words of the sung text. The Kathakali teacher learns to master the hand gestures and performs them in reverse, so that the learner does not see a mirror image, does not have to reverse the teacher's orientation, but imitates directly, i.e., the teacher's left-handed gesture is to be performed as a right-hand gesture by the learner. This helps the learner's body follow, as it is led by each gesture.

Pillai does not have to stand up to enact all the separate body parts. When, for example, with one hand, he shows the gesture of an elephant's trunk, Gokul responds not just with his one hand imitating the gesture of the trunk, but with his entire body following, helping create the form of an elephant; the right hand becomes the elephant's ear, the feet step rhythmically, slowly and heavily like an elephant's, the entire body sways majestically. For every gesture, the choreographed body, with the appropriate facial expressions and danced footsteps, follows. Besides hand gestural clues, facial expressions by the teacher also lead the learner, encouraging facial imitation. From my own experience, this helps the learner enter into the inner, subjective and emotional world of the characters he/she is learning.

The rhythm, beaten with a wooden stick on the wooden block placed in front of Pillai, is a cue for the feet and the danced steps. Each hand gesture, facial expression and the rhythm kept by the teacher is a cue for a complex and complete simulated action by the learner.

The teacher continues to sit through this entire process, only standing up to correct when an error is made. If the teacher is angry or upset with the learner, this standing up may suddenly become threatening. When not threatening, the sitting down–standing up relationship of the teacher and learner offers a stable and calm environment, even as the learner is empowered by being in a taller position than the teacher and looking down at the teacher.

Gokul is an excellent student and a star performer. In today's session, Pillai does not get angry even once. Gokul has been learning from Pillai for the past six years. You can feel their stable relationship while watching them. They work intensely, with great concentration, focus and pleasure. These are two bodies in communion with each other.

Kathakali's stable methodology of embodied transformation

To understand Kathakali's method of embodied transformation, I return to my observation of the one-on-one actor-training session. Pillai is teaching Gokul to play Bhīma, one of the five *pandava* brothers from the *Mahabharata* who, while travelling through the forest, is describing the animals he is seeing. Even as he describes these animals, he has to transform into them. This is how it plays out. Gokul as Bhīma sees an elephant and a python fighting. Gokul first becomes the elephant, wandering in the forest, breaking and eating branches with his trunk. Then Gokul becomes a watchful python seeing an elephant come his way. He then has to play both the elephant and the python as they fight. He then returns to playing the warrior, Bhīma. While there are codified gestures and conventions to help play and identify each animal/creature, these shifts in persona/character also demand body transformation. As an elephant, Gokul's body seems to fill out, expanding and growing larger than itself. As a python he seems to be constricting himself into a narrow space. His entire body seems engaged and transformed. Yet he moves out of one form into another with ease, with stability.

This stability of actor transformation in Kathakali training, I suggest, comes from knowing the body of the character or creature you are transforming into, at the first instance, as the body of the teacher. The teacher demonstrates and embodies each character. This embodiment the learner has observed, imitated, learnt and remembered. For Gokul, who has learnt this role from observing Pillai's body, Bhīma's body as it were, is Pillai's body. The elephant's body is also Pillai's body. The python's body too is Pillai's body.

To appreciate Kathakali body transformation techniques as different from other kinds of drama, I reference the example of scripted, realistic drama, as in the Stanislavskian magic "if" (Hapgood 1937:55) wherein the actor transforms by stepping into the shoes of a character who may not exist in the real space and with a real body. Rhonda Blair (1988), in her exploration of empathy and its neurological underpinnings, offers up the following example as an extreme end of such an empathetic transformation:

> Daniel Day Lewis … is said to stay "in character" from the beginning to the end of filming; but even so, this actor's choice is based on his sure knowledge

that he is not the character, and therefore must work consciously to maintain a connection to an alternative, temporary self.

(1988:92–103)

The return back from a temporary self to the real embodied self is always a delicate matter fraught with concern. Alternatively, other forms of performance offer the physical act of performing as a discovery of self, a process in which the actor, in personal terms, is behaving differently, as Richard Schechner elucidates:

> in personal terms, is "me behaving as if I am someone else" or "as if I am 'beside myself,' or 'not myself,'" as when in trance. But this "someone else" may also be "me in another state of feeling/being," as if there were multiple "me's" in each person.
>
> (1985:37)

Here, the actor is not in the shoes of another specific person/character, but is exploring and extending his sense of self to include other possible selves or other potential ways of being.

In Kathakali, a character's body exists through the teacher who embodies each character. The learner learns each character through the body transformation of/by the teacher. The clarity of this separation of the body of the learner from the body of the character helps create a stable objective engagement. The learner has his body, the character's body is clearly the Kathakali teacher's body. By this, the learner has a clear sense of both his own body, and the character's body. This clarity and stability are an aesthetic pleasure when the learner learns to transform from one to the other. Embodied actor transformation in Kathakali is, then, a pleasurable thing.

For the Kathakali learner and teacher, this stable shared objective world facilitates an experience of the more complex, shared subjective world of the Kathakali stories and characters. Three subjectivities are now at play: the learner's, the character's and the teacher's. This complex set of subjectivities flowers within the intimacy of the teacher–learner relationship. Learning is facilitated by an empathetic and sustained observation by the learner of the teacher's embodied demonstration and then a performance by the learner of the actions and emotions observed. For phenomenologist Husserl, this common world, this shared objectivity is arrived at or is made possible first of all by "empathy (Einfühlung), understood as the primordial experience of participating in the actions and feeling of another being without becoming the other" (1969:233). In Kathakali, actor training is a human craft though the characters played are gods and demons and epic heroes and heroines.

The *guru shishya* being-in-the-world, feet touching ritual

Watching Pillai and Gokul work together for an hour-and-a-half is a display of sustained observation by both learner and teacher. Gokul is very familiar with the gestures and the dance steps. He could easily remember them from memory and perform them independently. However, he watches Pillai intently throughout the session. Pillai too, through the hour-and-a-half, is watching Gokul intently even as he is performing the role himself, often in reverse, and often possessed by the emotional state of the character, as Gokul the learner is. With little shifts of the body, Pillai indicates changes in form, suggesting he is playing an elephant, and now a python. His face is animated and expressive. His feet are stamping the rhythm. Even as he is seated, he transforms into the elephant and the python. His seated body seems to expand and shrink, changing form. Throughout the enactment he continues to play the rhythm, beating the *talam* on the wooden block. His attention is both on his own body and the Kathakali form it is enacting, as well as on the learner. His concentration of attention seems to have no distraction, facilitating an intense learning session for Gokul.

Gokul ends the session by repeating the greeting ritual (now intended as a farewell) moving forward to touch Pillai's feet with his right hand. Pillai touches Gokul's head with his right hand and then gets up from the stool. This marks the end of the training session. Twice in the session, Gokul has touched Pillai's feet and twice has Pillai blessed him by touching his head. Gokul's respect for Pillai is actualised in each session with him touching Pillai's feet. A respect for the Kathakali teacher's body is an important element of the traditional *guru shishya* or master disciple relationship.

In questioning Pillai and Gokul around the practice of feet touching, I received similar answers. Both understood it as an expression of deep respect for the teacher. In their shared culture, Gokul and Pillai seemed to be at ease with both the objective behaviour of feet touching as with their subjective mental abstractions and meaning. However, for me, this practice is more problematic. This feet touching ritual is the kind of practice of the old social that I need to reconcile with for my work in the new social. I don't want students in Australia beginning and ending each session by touching my feet. I have felt a need to come up with an acceptable alternative.

This process of searching for a gestural transformation began for me after my student in Australia, Helen Smith, displayed her willingness to touch my feet as an expression of respect. Previous to this reflection, and under my guidance, both Helen Smith and Peter Fraser had been to India to learn from Pillai at the same International Centre for Kathakali, New Delhi. It was there that they too had witnessed the feet touching ritual. I asked Helen what this gesture signified for her:

Arjun: You seemed ok, willing to touch my feet?

Helen: Yes, this was after witnessing students doing it in India with Rajendran ji and other members of the ensemble, including musicians and singers. Even though it is not a custom in this country, I felt willing to do it as a mark of respect for your experience and teaching that you were so willing to share with us. I guess I was ready to do it because after years of living in other countries and trying on and trying out different customs, I am comfortable with difference. As there wasn't an equivalent gesture from my own culture that was a good match for the feeling of respect and gratitude, this one seemed like a good one to adopt.

Arjun: What did that gesture signify for you?

Helen: A mark of respect from a student to the master, the teacher. An acknowledgement that I have learnt a lot from you and still have a long way to go. A recognition of the fact that the source of creativity stems from the feet and that the energy arises out of the ground. A reminder of one's connection with the earth through the soles of the feet. By touching the feet perhaps it is an expression of a wish or desire to tap into the same creative force and source as that of the master's, as if "the magic" will somehow be transmitted from one to the other?

Later, in an email exchange, Helen added the following observations:

> It symbolizes a hierarchy, which cannot be reversed. In this instance, it is not bound by age ... I think I'm actually older than you! But more connected with a recognition of expertise and experience and possibly wisdom!! It is a gesture of trust: there's an unspoken acknowledgment of the power bestowed by the act.
> (Email to the author dated 11 July 2016)

In the present context of understanding the ritual of feet touching, Helen is presuming my acceptance of this cultural practice while, contrary to her abstractions, I am at odds with it. For example, I disagree with the almost mystical suggestion that "the source of creativity stems from the feet and that the energy arises out of the ground" (Helen's email, as cited above).[4] What does that actually mean? Instead, contradictorily, the feet, within the body hierarchy as circumscribed by Indian culture and the caste system, are the lowest part, and untouchable and impure. Within the context of my teaching Kathakali in Australia, Helen's touching of my feet then, for me, would be a display of her touching of what is my most "impure" socially available body part. By these opposing abstractions, I am compelled to renegotiate these actions and work to find new common ground of behaviour when teaching in Australia. In the new social, the actor-training space offers the potential for new negotiations which need to be explored. I use the example of feet touching to make complex and problematic the intercultural exchange of teaching the craft of acting of a sixteenth to seventeenth-century Indian form of dance drama to twenty-first-century contemporary western Australian actors. The body of the *guru* or master practitioner, its embodied self and encrypted culture is then placed centrally at the site of Kathakali actor training in Australia.

---

4 This mystification of the feet is often linked to a greater mystification, as it is done here by Schwartz. "Shiva Nataraja, literally Shiva as Lord of the Dance, actually dances the universe into being and then destroys it in the same way. The physical contact of the foot against the ground is sacred, for it precipitates existence. What is lifeless and dormant is animated by the touch of the foot; hence the soles of the dancers' feet are painted red, the auspicious color associated with growth and fertility. Hindu iconography pays considerable attention to the feet, for although they are the lowest part of the body, and thus in several ways the least elevated, they also connect the body to the sacred earth. When a shishya or student touches her guru's feet in humility and thanks, therefore, the act is meaningful on several levels" (2002:32).

3   From mythology to reality

Western perceptions of the exotic
Kathakali body

In my introductory workshop held in Melbourne, through a questionnaire handed out before we started, I explored the participants' knowledge, awareness and understanding of Kathakali dance drama. I found a set of expectations reflecting perceptions of an exotic otherness of the dance form. Most participants saw Kathakali as an "oriental" "religious" "spiritual" dance, popular for its "colours" and "costumes." In answers to more specific questions around its performativity, they highlighted the exotic elements – its hand gestures or *mudras*, its head-sliding movement, its flickering of eyebrows and its eye movements. Later, during the workshop, when I demonstrated, danced a short Kathakali *kalaasham* or danced a step for them and asked them to imitate and follow me they seemed to once again highlight its exotic otherness – making their eyes dance more than their bodies. This artificial imitation was especially evident when they videographed my demonstration and returned for the next session having independently created an artificial version of it, making it look more like a Bollywood dance than Kathakali (Figure 3.1).

Through the participants' initial exotic versions of the Kathakali form I understood what mimicry looked like. Rather than observe and imitate me carefully, they were playing out a vision of the orient from somewhere inside their minds. When I began to ask them to pay attention to my presence, to my actions, to what I was demonstrating to them, I could feel my tone becoming more stern, I could feel the presence of my teachers, I could hear them begin to speak through me. The moment I shifted the mood, demanding a more serious engagement, observation and enactment of the Kathakali form, the participants responded by asking me questions. Before performing every move they wanted me to explain it, to detail its sequencing verbally, before attempting to perform it.

I had a problem with this methodology. This was not the traditional method I was out to explore in the intercultural context of teaching Kathakali in Australia, and I did not want a mental engagement before an embodied interpretation. Aware of the notion of the western Cartesian mind/body split I was seeking to share a methodology received from my teachers, of leading, trusting and creating an embodied communion between master and pupil. The body of the eastern master practitioner brings an integrated body/mind to the site of actor training, and the eastern master is trained not to separate or hierarchise the body/mind of

Figure 3.1 The colourful make-up and costumes of the exotic: Kathakali Kari (Black) *veisham* (Kalamadalam Ramachandran). (Photo courtesy of Sreenath Narayan.)

the learner. It is for maintaining the body/mind integrity of the student that, at least in the initial process of learning the form, which may of course take a few years, the *guru* must lead, and lead by demonstrating and not by discussing. The pupil needs to mirror, to observe and imitate, to bring the mind to the embodied action, to its observation and enactment. This integrated psychophysicality of the eastern master practitioner leading the integrated psychophysicality of the pupil, through a process of mirroring, is the difference between the sociopsychophysical, and the psychophysical tradition, wherein a western teacher, having absorbed eastern techniques, works to integrate the Cartesian duality of the learner. Is the western teacher free of her own mind/ body split? In this context, in the following section I examine the scholarship of Phillip Zarrilli, the most prolific western academic writing on Kathakali, to further my argument for a valuing of the embodied presence of the eastern master or *guru* at the site of intercultural actor training.

The body of the Kathakali *guru* brings with it its embodied self and culture. In the second section of this chapter I engage with the work of theatre anthropologist and leading European interculturalist Eugenio Barba and share, through a reading of his work at the Odin Teatret, how the live presence of the eastern master, with its embodied self and culture, its performativity, may also complicate the intercultural exercise.

Phillip Zarrilli and the de-mystification of Kathakali

To make real, and move away from an exotic perception/representation of Kathakali I first examine the work of Phillip Zarrilli (1984, 2000A&B, 2004, 2009, 2011, 2013), the most prolific academic writing on Kathakali, who later developed his psychophysical approach to actor training. In this section I contextualise Zarrilli's scholarship, documenting a departure from what I argue is the sociopsychophysicality of Kathakali, to what he evolves over time and frames as "Psychophysical Acting" (2009).

Zarrilli's scholarly engagement may be arranged chronologically, from the anthropological/ethnographic (1984, 2000a), to the phenomenological (2004) and on to the intercultural and psychophysical (2009, 2011, 2013). For this author's frame of the sociopsychophysical, amidst all his writings, it is Zarrilli's practice-led enquiry of his relationship with his *kalaripayyattu guru* in "Embodying the Lion's 'fury'" (2000b) that is most inspiring.

In his opening chapters of *The Kathakali Complex, Actor, Performance and Structure* (1984) Zarrilli sets out to demystify Kathakali and see it as a six-teenth- to seventeenth-century dance theatre from the southernmost state of India, Kerala.

De-Mystifying Kathakali

The late sixties provided an arena ripe for the development of these "mys-teries" of Kathakali, as yoga, the "wisdom of the east," "spirituality," and "altered states of consciousness" became passwords to a tolerable existence. Such general cultural phenomenon, coupled with the writings of Barba and Iyer, Grotowski's reference, the new attention given to Artaud's "Theatre of Cruelty," as well as interpretations of Genet's work as a "Theater of Ritual," brought to Western theater the dubious merit of searching for experimental stimulation through ritual and myth. It was a prime moment for the creation of a self-fulfilling prophecy, for a popular image to envelop a foreign dra-matic form, which could fulfill the yearning of a culture desperately in search of mystical-ritualistic roots.

(Zarrilli 1984:6)

Countering the European mystification of Kathakali, Zarrilli sets out to describe what Kathakali is.

Kathakali traditionally enacts texts (attakathas) based on India's great epics, The Mahabharata, Ramayana and the Puranas. Until recently all the plays of the Kathakali repertory were based on these sources. Kathakali perfor-mances of these dramatized stories are best described as dance-dramas-a blend of dance, acting and music in an integrated whole. Like many other Asian and Indian forms of performance it may be called a form of "total" theater.

(1984:7)

A "total" theatre is worthy of a sustained inquiry and Zarrilli responds with over two decades of academic engagement with Kathakali actor training. In the following sections I will sample some of the ways Zarrilli's scholarship marks a departure, away from the sociopsychophysicality of Kathakali towards the psychophysical. To reiterate an important distinction, in the psychophysical, it is a western teacher who absorbs eastern practices, and then leads the students in a workshop mode of performer training. The absence of the eastern master practitioner or *guru* effects a significant departure from a sociopsychophysical culture of duality/joint action, towards an interest in the individual mind/body psychophysical. I trace in Zarrilli's early scholarship the genesis of this separation, and briefly detail its consequence.

Zarrilli and his mind/body duality

In *Psychophysical Acting: An Intercultural Approach after Stanislavski* (2009), Zarrilli, working within the embodiment paradigm while using the human body as a tool of enquiry, reflects back on his own Cartesian mind/body separation. I quote him extensively as it is important for my critique to locate the embodied compulsions and conditions he brings to his early scholarship. Here he is simultaneously reflecting on his body, trained in American schools and colleges, to aggressively win in sports, even while mentally/philosophically, he was trying to become a pacifist.

> But my body remained separate, that is, it would not be "pacified." It had been shaped by a masculine culture of the body which assumed an overarching and directive "will" which, through sheer determination and/or aggression, could shape the body per se, and/or make use of the body to impose that will on someone/something else. As my body was a "thing" to be mastered, male culture gave me permission to keep this body sequestered and separate from my beliefs and values. Separate from my biomedical/sports body, I inhabited an other body, the personal and private body which was a repository of my feelings. It too existed in a state of tension with my beliefs and ethical values, and also remained separate from my biomedical/sports body. My (separate) mind was manifest in my will to mastery, in my reflexive consciousness which could watch my sports body from the outside and in my beliefs and values which attempted, through my active will, to impose themselves on either or both bodies.
>
> (Zarrilli 2009:23)

Zarrilli's aggressions with his "sport body" later extend to an initial six-month learning engagement with *meyyarappu*, Kathakali's *kalaripayattu*-inspired body exercise routine, followed by a seven-year engagement with the Kerala martial art form itself. Practitioner led explorations of Kathakali texts, character, subjectivity and sociology, were not a part of his research-the academic enquiry was based on more traditional ethnographic methods.

Left- and right-side stage conventions

A careful study of Zarrilli's early scholarship on Kathakali (1984) raises certain issues of selective interpretation. As an example, while describing Kathakali stage conventions Zarrilli (1984) records the codes around the staging of characters but describes values connected to only one side – the right side of the convention. The following is his description.

> When two characters are onstage together, the use of the stage is generally governed by the socially accepted preeminence and "cleanliness" of the right side over the left. In daily life the right side is the side of respect and one eats only with the right "clean" hand. This social convention is reflected in the fact that on the Kathakali stage the right side (stage right, to the audience's left facing the stage) is always the side of respect. The character of higher status will normally be on the stage right side, with the character of lower status to his left. For example when Bhīma and Panchali are onstage together in Kalyana Saugandhikam Bhīma will be stage right and Panchali stage left. As male and husband Bhīma is of higher status and his wife remains to his left.
>
> (Zarrilli 1984:165)

While detailing the location and values of the right side as "preeminence," "cleanliness," "respect," Zarrilli, besides highlighting a difference in status, neglects to describe/explore/balance the logic and values of the right with the left side – for example not detailing the left as unclean, dirty, contempt worthy, impure, polluted. As he observes, the convention between husbands and wives has the husband standing on the right side with the wife on the left side of the stage. More generally, the left space is occupied by the wives/ females/lower-status/lower-caste characters. In the Kathakali classic *kalayana saugandhikam* or The Flower of Good Fortune, besides the example of husband and wife, there is another scene where Hanuman the monkey god turns himself into a dirty old monkey and purposefully crosses over from the right side of the stage, to lie down on the left side. From monkey god on the right side, to dirty old monkey on the left side. Bhīma, the warrior, stands on the right side and with contempt calls him *vanaradhama* or the lowest of monkeys. When he approaches him he indicates to the audience, using hand gestures, that the monkey "smells," is unclean, impure. The left side as a site for the unclean, inferior, impure is as well-established a convention as those values that govern the right. In terms of social hierarchy, a messenger, a lower-caste character, for example, will stand on the left side, the King, on the right. Zarrilli seems to respond to the right side but stops short of exploring the values of the left side, and the interrelationship of the left with the right.

I do of course recognise the difficulty of ethnographically gathering left-side data. Evoor Rajendran Pillai, in an interview conducted by me at the International Centre for Kathakali in New Delhi on the 26 August, 2016, answered my question on the left–right division of the Kathakali stage with the example of receiving an honoured guest on the appropriate side. Pointing to the right side of the stage he suggested that it was there, on the right side, that you would seat the guest.

On being asked where he would seat a dishonoured guest he just laughed off my enquiry. Knowing the culture I found it inappropriate to confront him further about something he seemed to not want to talk about – for example, to engage further with ideas of impurity and pollution and to indicate the connection of the impure left side with the status of women.

It is this difficulty of gathering left-side data that has made me seek the conceptual over the empirical as a method to reveal, for example, in Chapter 6 the social weave of caste and untouchability. In these situations I also found the auto-ethnographic methodology both a problematic conflicting tool (as it drew in my own caste status) as well as conceptually, a valuable asset. It is my embodied knowledge and lived experience that allow me to highlight the absent uncleanliness of the left side and its social consequence. Zarrilli, like

Figure 3.2 The left side: *Stree Veisham* or female character (Margi Vijaykumar). (Photo courtesy of Sreenath Narayan.)

I was, would have been told about the values of the right side of the convention and not of the left side. His scholarship could then be seen as right side–centric, with the left side of the living caste-encrypted social body neglected. This neglect is attended to in part by Marlene Pitkow through her PhD thesis titled *Representations of the Feminine in Kathakali Dance-Drama* (1998) and through her excellent article "The Good, the Bad and the Ugly: Kathakali's Females and the Men who Play them" (2011:223–243) and by Daugherty and Pitkow with the appropriately titled "Who Wears the Skirts in Kathakali?" (1988:138–156). My own work with the sociopsychophysical, through an integration of the social with the psychophysical, attempts to balance the left and right side. The social includes both, the world of the left side, the feminine and lower castes that occupy it, and the right side, the masculine, upper and dominant castes including the *nair* warriors who performed both *kalaripayyatu* and Kathakali (Figure 3.2).

A separation of the internal and external processes of actor training

Following up on complications of the left- and right-side stage convention, I address a different kind of separation, one between master and pupil. In his analysis of Kathakali acting Zarrilli says, "Kathakali acting is both an external and internal process. The external or technical aspect of performance is the beginning place of training" (1984:207). Here he is alluding to the student's external objectification of *bhava* or embodied emotional states:

> Even though emotional states are extremely important in Kathakali, these emotional states are objectified and *not* personalized expressions. We have seen how the internal side of training begins when a teacher may ask to draw on his own experience. Notice that the student is *not* being asked to *begin* inside his personal feelings. His personal feelings are not the point of origin for the external action. Rather the neophyte *begins with the form*, the external facial gestures in the expression of emotional states.
>
> (1984:209)

Zarrilli's perception of Kathakali emotional states as "objectified and not personalized expressions" (ibid.:209) suggests a disengagement with the personal, individual and psychological, values precious to western performers. For Zarrilli the student seems to be making external facial gestures with no inner personal connection. However, I argue, for child actors, the personal, individual and psychological is a complex process that requires greater understanding of what constitutes personal feelings. In this long-term master pupil relationship the formal and objectified have embedded into them the personal, and in reverse, the personal has within it the formal. This is true for the *guru* who, from years of practice and performance, includes the subjective in every outward expression and demonstration, and for the learner, who observes and absorb this skill. The internal external binary is reductive for at no point of the learning curve are the personal and the formal separated. The moment a master accepts a pupil the bond becomes an intimate personal one.

In further support of valuing the pupil's personal and subjective I reference here Eugenio Barba's brief but poetic understanding of the Kathakali learning process expressed in his article "On the Steps on the Riverbank" (1994) about his three-week stay at the Kerala Kalamandalam. He says of the young students learning Kathakali:

> There is a difference in the theater you begin to practice as an adult and the theater whose apprenticeship begins in childhood. The children are projected into a context that gives them a value, into a tradition that transcends them, a tradition that at first they do not grasp, but little by little, gets incorporated into them. They feel they represent something beyond them, a higher meaning.
>
> In Cheruthuruthy, the value of the theater did not lie in what the children may have said, believed or dreamed. It was as though they were carrying on their frail shoulders, sometimes with difficulty, sometimes lightheartedly, the image of a tradition they might later interpret and transform.
>
> (Barba 1994:107)

Barba's vision of the Kathakali students is deeply evocative of the interiority, subjectivity and the depth of self suggested in the student's care and absorption into the Kathakali form. As part of a living tradition a Kathakali student would have seen many Kathakali performances, would have the vision of his own culture, a vision of the heroic warrior Bhīma, the monster Baka, the magnificently attired monkey god Hanuman, the majestic lion, the proud elephant and the dazzling peacock. All these wonderful images would have enriched the six/seven/eight-year-old's inner eye and inner being, enriching his subjective personal self. The objectified training process only then adds to the subjective vision. The embodied object is brought alive by the personal within, the personal as defined by a vision of the historical, cultural inheritance.

As a child of six growing up in New Delhi (even though I came to Kathakali later in life, and on my return from England at the age of 24), I knew the entire Mahabharata by heart. Every episode, every character and every conflict. Well almost! My father's sister, a young widow, spent her winter afternoons reading the original Mahabharata in Sanskrit, and, as I was Arjun, engaged me in these passionate stories about Arjuna and his brothers, the Pandavas. Having my own real brother named Yudhishthira, the eldest Pandava, helped me imagine the Pandavas as my family. These were stories and characters that were imprinted deep in my childhood imagination. When I began learning Kathakali, this ancient personal space within was tapped and became the source for a rich subjectivity, even as I, as a matured adult, slowly and painstakingly began working on the form. I remember the first time when I played Bhīma, Arjuna's brother in the Mahabharata, I felt an amazing, deep and true emotion of love for this big bumbling powerful Pandava brother who was now within me. I had never before (or have since) experienced an equivalent feeling. Perhaps this is what Barba meant by the "invisible" in the following letter, appropriately to Zarrilli:

> When I claim that theatrical work consists fundamentally in rendering the invisible visible, I am speaking of something completely different: I am investigating that process by means of which mental energy (invisible) becomes somatic energy (visible).
>
> (Barba 1988:7–14)

Perhaps the wonderful space of the child's imagination is an element of that invisible force that exists within the depths of our subjectivity.

In contrast, the separation of the internal from the external seems to keep apart that magical space of the child's subjective. Zarrilli holds on to this framing even 16 years later in *Kathakali Dance Drama: Where Gods and Demons Come to Play* (2000a:69) when he elaborates quite extensively on the internal external theme. However, in his notes to the same work he seems to qualify this long-held perspective. He writes "I have placed quotation marks around 'external' and 'internal' since using the term suggests a dualism that is inappropriate to the dialectic between these two modes of actualization, both equally integral to the actor's process" (2000a:216).

The sociopsychophysical paradigm addresses this dialectic, highlighting the centrality of the joint action between master and pupil. This joint action works at a communion, and not an internal external separation, right from the initiation of the relationship, to the full flowering when the pupil becomes a *guru* herself. For this author, it is when in "Embodying the Lion's 'Fury'" (2000b) Zarrilli turns to examine his relationship with his own *kalaripayattu guru* that a stable, deeply insightful sociopsychophysical scholarship is on offer. In it he describes brilliantly the moment when he sees in his teacher's eye, "the lion's fury," the clarity of a warrior's intention to kill. It is only the practitioner researcher exploring his relationship with his *guru* who can, as a practitioner, come up so close to that kind of powerful gaze, and then return as a scholar, to share it with the reader. The *guru shishya* facilitates such intimacy of knowing.

In the land of *advaita* or the belief in the unity of all experience, in the unity of the *atma* (individual spirit) with the *paramatma* (supreme spirit) or the self with the greater self, a concentration on the learner's individual psycho/physical internal/external body/mind duality as separate from the teacher's, is a departure from the essence of the tradition. While philosophical concepts like *advaita* and *atma-paramatma*, and the religious and spiritual culture they evoke, may seem abstract, religious and mystical they play out in ordinary living even for example through the offering of a sustained teacher student relationship. It is an ordinary idea in traditional Indian culture to seek a *guru* or teacher and then stay unified or loyal to that relationship for years if not a lifetime. I too learnt Kathakali from Sadanam Balakrishnan for 10 years and from Evoor Rajendran Pillai intermittently for another 14 years. The older traditional culture facilitates these bonds and their sustenance over lengths of time.[1] The psychophysical tradition, through a replacement of the eastern master with the western teacher, separates the pupil, the form and technique, from the body of the *guru*. This separation may be perceived as reductive.

Kathakali and the Natyashastra

Having problematised the idea of "separation," I now work to detail another marker of the Cartesian mind/body split, a reflex for "hierarchizing" (Leder 1990:4).[2] I use the knowledge available from an embodied traditional practitioner like Balakrishnan to reference Zarrilli's scholarship on the role of the Natyashastra. Both Zarrilli (1984) and Balakrishnan (2005) begin their thesis on Kathakali by identifying its sources and attempting to put it into a historic context. Significantly their first difference is on one of the assumed, primary textual source of Kathakali, the Natyashastra. While Zarrilli aligns and connects Kathakali along a straight historical line that emerges from the Natyashastra in the 2nd century AD, reaching Kathakali via the classical form *kutiyattam* (1984:39), Balakrishnan articulates a need to distance Kathakali from it.

> For instance, the founders of Kathakali had a wealth of local dramatic examples from which to draw upon and hence have bypassed many of the tenets of the Natya Sastra, the most important Sanskrit treatise on Indian theater.
>
> (2005:27)

Balakrishnan's need to define and distance Kathakali's relationship with the Natyashastra makes him drive the argument further. "In fact, the similarities that do exist between Bharata Muni's treatise and Kathakali are fewer than expected and possibly incidental" (2005:27).

Balakrishnan's struggles with the Natyashastra are relevant as they reveal local, regional, internal schisms and stresses within the nation state. Since Independence in India in 1947, an overriding national agenda has meant the recognition and celebration of iconic texts like the Natyashastra as a part of the pan-Indian national identity. At times this national agenda is perceived to dominate the local. Balakrishnan, an embodied practitioner, responding to his local Kerala roots and identity, while resisting an obligatory acknowledgement of the Natyashastra as a primary source of the classical arts including Kathakali, suggests that the sources of Kathakali lie more practically within the embodied practices of indigenous

---

1 For a more critical commentary on the *guru shishya* in Kathakali as a hierarchical unequal power-based and iniquitous system read (Narayanan 2016:231–242). This book examines the well-functioning relationship but acknowledges the opposite, one that exploits the power unbalance.

2 Leder suggests a separation of mind and body has "far-reaching social effects" (1990:4). These "social effects" set up for Leder concerns ethical in nature with the Cartesian hierarchical dualism sub serving "projects of oppression directed towards women, animals, nature, and other 'Others'" (ibid.:4).

folk, ritual, tribal *and* classical performing traditions of Kerala including, and he names all of the following (in addition to Theyyam, Mutiyettu and Kalaripayatuu),

> Purkkali, Kaikoottikkali, Kolkali, Panemkali, Margamkali, Kaniarkali, Mangalamkali, Chimmanamkali, Velakali, Tattinmelkoothu, Pavakoothu, Chakyarkoothu, Kolamtullal, Ottantullal, Patayani, Kotamoori, Arjun Nrittam and Tolpava Koothu.

> (2005:27)

Zarrilli on the other hand while acknowledging the maze of performance traditions and sources in Kerala does not choose to name or engage with them in great detail and instead hierarchises the classical, defining it as aesthetically the most refined – "the classical performance tradition is the most aesthetically refined of these performance spheres"(1984:39). He further gives the Natyashastra its place of pride right at the apex of an entire series/set/range of texts and performance traditions.

> The classical performance tradition of Kerala and all India is based on the principles and techniques encoded in Bharata's Natyashastra, the encyclopedia of Indian dramaturgy and theatrical technique (200 B.C–200 A.D).

> (Zarrilli 1984:39)

While Balakrishnan roots the source of an important element of Kathakali performativity, the language of gestures, to a regional text, Hastalakhsdeepika (2005:134), Zarrilli, even while contradicting himself, declares the source of the language of gestures as the Natyashastra:

> Kathakali's language of gesture, another building block of the actor's basic technique, is part of Kathakali's inheritance of the classic tradition from the Natyashastra through *Kutiyattam*. Both Kathakali and *Kutiyattam's* hand gesture languages are based upon a regional text, the Hastalaksanadipika, a catalogue of the basic hand poses with lists of words, which that hand pose represents. While there is a common heritage to the two gestural languages, over the years a number of variations have developed. A comparison of Kathakali gestures with those recorded in the ninth chapter of the Natyashastra would also reveal numerous differences in the basic set of root gestures. Despite these differences and variations, Kathakali's gestural language has its origins in the Natyashastra tradition and maintains in its own system the same basic function as in the original system. (1984:126–127)

Later, Zarrilli has had a rethink and is more circumspect. In his notes to *Kathakali Dance Drama: Where Gods and Demons Come to Play* (2000) he writes:

> 7.While the rasa/bhava aesthetic and the Natyashasthra can be described as pan-Indian, the [*sic*] therefore as formative in the history of Indian poetics and

dramaturgy, the ways in which this aesthetic and its correlative concepts such as "appropriateness" are realized are always context- and genre-specific and therefore are always unique and historically specific. Even though *kutiyattam* has played an extremely important role in kathakali's development, each contribution from *kutiyattam* has been adapted, however subtly, to kathakali's unique performance structure and version of this aesthetic. Therefore I have been careful to use the key qualifying terms "based on" because kathakali's version of "appropriateness" and the rasa/bhava aesthetic are unique.[3]

(2000:215)

If the above stated, "appropriateness and the rasas/bhava aesthetic are unique," as Zarrilli seems to acknowledge, then why source them back to the Natyashastra? In contrast, Balakrishnan works to define in great detail one of the significant sources of Kathakali, *theyyam*, a ritual performance by lower-caste and untouchable performers: "The eight caste communities – the Velan, Kopalan, Parayan, Mayilon, Munnuttan, Anhuttan, Malayan and Vannan" (2005:29). He further defines the castes that perform the three categories of *theyyam*. The first category – the "Velan, Kopalan, Parayan and Mayilon" (2005:30). The second category – the "Parayan, Malayan, Munnuttan, Anhuttan and Vannan" (2005:31). The third – the "Vannan and Malayan" (2005:32).

This naming, detailing of caste is significant in understanding the art of the performer in the context of his or her being in the world and further being in their own art form. In *kutiyattam* the upper-caste temple servant's body chants and recites text (Balakrishnan 2005:61–72). In Kathakali (Zarrilli 1984, Balakrishnan 2005) the *nair* warrior caste's body is silent, not chanting or speaking but dancing vigorously to sung text. In *theyyam*, the "untouchable's" body goes into a trance and dances and walks and talks freely as if possessed by the temple deity, possessing a heightened "touchability" for a day or two (Balakrishnan 2005:29–42). While traditionally *kutiyattam* is restricted to the temple because of the existential status of the upper-caste temple servants, and *theyyam* is in some measure restricted both to the temple and to a brief season in the year due to the restrictions placed on the free movement/existence of the lower castes, Kathakali is able to both step away from any restriction of place, by performing outside the temple, and of time, by performing through the entire year. Aesthetically too Kathakali has been influenced by these art forms. "Kathakali took body exercises from Kalaripayat its Abhinaya from Kutiyattam and its Kalashams, make up, costumes, battle scenes between good and evil from Teyyam" (Zarrilli 1984:43).

In this crisscrossing of cultures, castes and communities, any attempt at a hierarchising of aesthetic refinement can be problematic. Zarrilli uses the formal measure of a "developed and exclusive codified language" and "refinement in nuance of technique" (1984:40) as factors suggestive of the superior refinement

---

3 D. Appukuttan Nair provides a comprehensive discussion of the differences between Kathakali's realisation of this aesthetic and what is found in the Natyasastra (Nair and Paniker 1993:6–9)

of the classical arts. Almost immediately, Zarrilli does qualify his declaration of the superior refinement of the classical arts with a reiteration of the cross-cultural influence and similarity between the classical, the folk and the ritualistic, concluding, "Classical performances are not necessarily MORE complex than ritual or folk performances. They each embody their own form of complexity" (1984:41).

The sophistication of the untouchable *theyyam* performer

In support of the above- articulated stance, of an equalising of the aesthetic refinement of these varied art forms, I take time here to describe an aspect of *theyyam*'s sophistication. *Theyyam* is a ritualistic performance in which the performer during the course of an annually held performance becomes the temple deity, bringing alive the deity, representing the deity for the worshippers. The worshipping village folk believe the deity extremely powerful and dangerous, if displeased, and consequently all the preparatory rites and rituals are painfully and precisely executed for fear of retribution. As can be imagined the make-up and costume are detailed and laborious as an ordinary mortal is transformed into a god. When it is finished and the performer looks into the mirror, performative magic begins. Balakrishnan describes the untouchable actor's transformation into a deity, god:

> After the final touches to the make up, usually the application of lip color, the dancer looks into the hand held mirror handed to him by his assistants. The magnificent, colossal form of the deity is reflected—the deity has become manifest in the performer. The dancer plucks flowers from the wristlets or headdress and offers them to the deity reflected in the mirror. Instantly, he falls into a trance and the dance of the Theyyam begins.
>
> (2005:35)

What can be more refined and sophisticated than the ability to enter into a trance, to be instantaneously transformed into the other? To become a god for a day! To play, dance, move, speak and behave like a god. Without error. Perfectly. And the return from this possessed state? How does that happen? Balakrishnan explains: "It is believed that the actor who takes the role of Kali becomes so entranced that he may, indeed, kill Darika if not stopped by the removal of her headgear, the Muti" (2005:51).

Here is a critical element of the body in performance. The head. And the headdress, the *muti* or the *kiridam* as it is also called in Kathakali. With its removal the trance ends. Both the wearing of, and the taking off, of the headdress are important events, at the start and end of the trance/possession/performance state. The headdress forces a significant balance to the head preventing the performer from "losing his head" as he goes deeper into the trance/performance. The *kiridam* helps facilitate this performance state. Very few western performers have ever danced Kathakali with a *kiridam*. It is my experience that a balanced head is the precondition for the flow of emotions, for the *bhava* or embodied emotion to be experienced by the actor. Perhaps, when the head/brain is stable and safe, emotions flow. Evoor Rajendran Pillai, in an interview conducted on the 26 August, 2016 at the International Centre for Kathakali, reaffirmed for me the importance of the *kiridam*, suggesting that every element of the initial training is geared towards the control and balance of the body working towards the balancing of the *kiridam*.

In his teaching sessions I observed he makes sure that the body is perfectly balanced, a movement to the right side is measured and balanced with an exact movement to the left side. This habit, of perfectly matching the left- and right-side movements, works to keep the head centred and balanced, allowing later, in performance, for the *kiridam* to sit with ease on the head. It is this balanced head and body that becomes a vessel to be filled with emotion. Thus the wearing of the *kiridam* is critical to the performer's own and the audience's experience of aesthetic pleasure or *rasa*. This wearing of a *kiridam* or some form of elaborate head-dress/crown is common to all three forms – *kuddiyattam*, *kathakali* and *theyyam* – making all three equally sophisticated modes of performance.

In a world made complex by a multiplicity of cultures co-existing and jostling with each other for space and influence, further complicated by issues of language and translation, however well-intentioned the western practitioner is, as exampled in the present instance by Zarrilli's reflex to hierarchise and elevate the classical, he/she is vulnerable to the embodied compulsions of his/her own "habitus" (Bourdieu 1990:52–65). This reflex to separate and hierarchise has consequences, directly or indirectly, for the subject researched, as revealed by Balakrishnan's need to renegotiate and de-elevate the influence of the Natyashastra on his art form.

It is to heal the western actor's psycho physical or mind/body split that, at the first instance, the psychophysical tradition engages with the eastern arts. The eastern *guru* or master practitioner brings to the table, as it were, an integrated body/mind that is deeply trained not to separate and hierarchise the learner's body/mind, but instead teach it to commune with itself, to integrate. This presence of the master practitioner or *guru*'s body at the site of actor training is the essence of the sociopsychophysical tradition, as different to the psychophysical, which is often led by a western practitioner who has absorbed eastern practices for a while but may still be negotiating a mind/body split.

The live presence of the eastern master's body, with its embodied self and culture, its performativity, however, holds potential to complicate the intercultural psychophysical exercise, as the next section examining the work of Eugenio Barba illustrates.

Eugenio Barba and the Odin Teatret

For a practice-led research project working to reconcile the practices of one culture (Indian) within another (Australian), Eugenio Barba's ambitious, wide-ranging and sustained anthropological research on eastern and western modes of performance, including Kathakali, demands special focus and attention. Eugenio Barba's Odin Teatret was created in Oslo, Norway, in 1964, and moved to Holstebro, Denmark, in 1966. Its performance history records a significant and successful body of work with 76 productions, performed in 63 countries and in different social contexts. Barba's expertise of intercultural exchange, techniques of performance, cross-disciplinary endeavours and international collaboration is well-established and institutionalised with the International School of

Theatre Anthropology (ISTA). From its initially precarious origins, as Bharucha's research suggests (1993:54–67), Barba moved, after a 20-year-long struggle, to head a state-supported Teaterlaboratorium with a grant of $250,000 (Bharucha 1993:65), a significant sum of money in the early 1990s. In 2019–2020, Barba is still very active and influential in the intercultural actor-training space.

Barba's anthropological research had its origins in the practical needs of actor training for the theatre. Over the years of working with his actors at the Odin Teatret, Eugenio Barba observed that some actors were good performers but not good in training, while others were good in training but were not good in performance. After extensive work and research, he concluded that it was not relevant whether the actors were good in performance or good in training or good in both. What was relevant was that all actors must enhance and train their "scenic presence, i.e., their ability to attract an audience's attention by their sheer presence" (Barba 1995:9). This presence then allowed their minutest of actions to be of interest to an audience. This, Barba concluded, the actors do by making extra daily actions. These extra daily physical and vocal exertions are based on principles different from those that govern daily behaviour. Through transcultural analysis, by mapping training and performance techniques of a wide range of traditions, Barba was able to single out "recurring principles" (9) or "shared themes of performativity." These recurring principles were to be used by Odin Teatret actors as points of departure, away from the source traditions and towards a new, individualised way of working.

Here is Barba sharing the genesis of this process, of his discovery of the recurring principles:

> In 1978, the actors all left Holstebro in search of stimuli which might help them shatter the crystallization of behavior, which tends to form in every individual or group. For three months, they dispersed in all directions: to Bali, India, Brazil, Haiti and Struer, a small town about fifteen kilometers from Holstebro. The pair who had gone to Struer to a school of ballroom dancing learned the tango, Viennese waltz, foxtrot and quickstep. Those who had gone to Bali studied baris and legong; the one who had been in India, kathakali; the two who had visited Brazil, capoera and candomble dances. They had all stubbornly insisted on doing what, in my view, ought absolutely to be avoided: they had learned styles – that is, the results of other people's techniques.
>
> (6)

While watching his actors perform these newly and hurriedly learnt exotic acting skills and techniques, Barba had a moment of truth, an epiphany. He noticed his actors putting on another skin/skeleton in order to perform, for example, their version of a Balinese dance or Kathakali. However, when the performance ended they would seem to step out of it and step back into their Odin Teatret actor skin/skeleton. And yet, in the passage from one skeleton/skin to another, in spite of the difference in expressivity, they applied similar principles.

These recurring principles were to become the basis of the work ahead. As he observes:

This "putting on" and "taking off", this change from a daily body technique to an extra-daily body technique and from a personal technique to a formalized Asian, Latin American or European technique, forced me to ask myself a series of questions which led me into new territory.

(6)

This new territory was the work of the unique individualised way of the Odin Teatret. This way used the recurring principles as points of departure, away from the source tradition; not a surface, artificial wearing of a few learnt techniques from another culture, as at least the actor who had gone to India to learn Kathakali seemed to demonstrate.

A video recording exists of the Kathakali-inspired performance created by this Odin Teatret actor who learnt Kathakali for three months in India. The excerpt can be found in the Odin Teatret's 1979 performance of *The Million* (1979), created in 16 mm film with a video copy available online.[4] Produced by Odin Teatret Film, relevant footage runs from 4:15 to 11:50. I viewed this video very carefully, stopping and starting many times, to note down all the Kathakali elements in the dance. I observed formal Kathakali conventions and steps, mixed up with interpretive and creative additions by the performer. I noted these down in my diary and then framed a response to this viewing, set out below:

The Million is about Marco Polo's journey to the east. A performer sits on stage as Marco Polo. A kind of strange sensational orientalist fantasy world of song and dance plays around him. The audience sits on the ground, in a round. After about six to seven minutes a performer emerges dancing and dressed up as a character that I recognise as a Kathakali character *pootna*, the demoness, transformed into a beautiful woman and sent to murder the baby god Krishna. As she starts dancing I recognise Kathakali steps, gestures, feminine movements as well as eye movements and facial expressions. The performer displays a rough elementary skill and control over the Kathakali form. To that he adds his own Chaplinesque kind of artificial stylised energy with jerky, mechanical movements. Is this a parody, a conscious mocking of the Kathakali form? I am open to that thought, to that conscious playful affront. However, my fears rise to the surface. I know the story. It is *pootna moksham*,[5] the liberation of the demoness named *pootna*. It is the

---

4 A copy of the video can be bought and downloaded from www.artfilms.com.au/item/odin-teatret-th e-million.

5 For anyone familiar with Kathakali and especially with actor training, this story of *Pootna Moksham* is often the first story, after the initial dance steps that are taught to a western performer coming to India to learn Kathakali. Being a *stree vesham* or a female role, it does not have the heavy *kiridam* (worn only by male characters) nor the heavy costume with the layers of cloth making up the billowing "skirt." In Kathakali actor training, this story of *Pootna* is not really taught in the formal rehearsal spaces. It is learnt by sheer observation of other senior performers performing it. The learner is challenged by primary techniques and skills. This is why it is taught to "westerners" who are there briefly, to learn Kathakali for a few weeks to a few months.

story around the birth of the Hindu god Krishna. A story similar to baby Jesus and Herod, for it has been predicted that Krishna will grow up to kill *kamsa*, the King. To prevent this, *kamsa* sends the demoness to kill baby Krishna. Dressed as a beautiful woman, Pootna arrives at Krishna's home and manages to feed him milk from her poison smeared breasts. However, instead of being killed, Krishna sucks both the poisoned milk as well as the life out of Pootna. In the Odin Teatre performance, as in the Kathakali performance, a baby doll is brought in and placed on the ground. After dancing a mock, strange and frenzied version of Kathakali, the performer suddenly stamps on this doll with his right foot, stamps on baby Krishna!

(Recorded in my diary on 1 December, 2014)

To clarify, the Odin Teatret audience has no way of knowing the baby doll represents a god named Krishna as there is no dialogue and no storyline to this show. One scene flows into another, like an oriental fantasy. The actor, however, would of course have known what he was doing. What was he trying to achieve by stamping on another culture's god? Or, was the performer creating a new interpretation, with Pootna killing off Krishna quickly, even before he had a chance to kill her? That could indeed be a new, humorous twist to the story.

The performance itself, as Barba had predicted, was a superficial adoption of certain techniques of another culture, a comic caricature, a Frankenstein-like horror show for me. It seemed to have come from a Kathakali form, learnt in a terrible hurry. However, my interest in this foot stamping of a god is not to critique Barba's theatre nor to research the inner logic of a European theatre and its transcultural experiments. My concern rather is with another matter: what an analysis of this action helps me enquire into and reveal about the embodiment of Indian culture and its representation outside of India. I am using these representations of Indian culture in Europe not to get to the root of their authenticity, but to assist me in conceiving my arguments as they evolve through my practice-led research.

It is my lived experience with Indian culture that informs my reaction to his stamping of the doll Krishna. The foot is the least sacred, the most profane part of the body. If accidently your foot touches another's body, you touch your hand to their body and then to your head as if compensating for the foot touch with a head touch. As children we were made to do this gesture of repentance and not just to a body but even to a book. If one accidently touched a book with the foot, the book would immediately need to be touched by the hand and then that hand touched to the head. Taboos about the foot are an intrinsic part of Indian culture. In my home here in Australia, guests take their shoes off before entering the house. This is of course as much about the house being kept clean as it is about it being kept sacred.

A foot-centric conflict

The Odin Teatret performer's foot stamping leads this foot-centric story to another stamping or, more precisely, the kicking of a book, that became an issue between

Barba and founder member Indian Odissi dance *guru* Sanjukta Panigrahi. Here is one of the leading actresses of the Odin Teatret, Julia Varley, recounting a specific incident while speaking of Panigrahi's work with the Odin Teatret. I examine this incident and her role in it both for her presence as a master practitioner and for her embodiment of Indian culture as reflected in the conflicting situation Varley describes:

> On another occasion Sanjukta refused to follow Eugenio's instructions. It was during the ISTA in Salento, Italy, in 1987. Goethe's Faust was being worked on. Faust was represented by Katsuko Azuma, Margarita by the Onnagata Kanichi Hanayagi and Sanjukta was Mephistopheles, dressed in European style for the first time and, also for the first time, with her long hair let down loose. At a certain point a book fell from Faust's hands and Sanjukta, as Mephistopheles, had to kick it away. To mistreat a book was taboo in her culture and so she refused. Despite all of her solidarity towards Eugenio and towards the work in which she was discovering the richness of silence as accompaniment, she categorically refused to kick the book.
>
> (1998:249–273)

Present now in the cauldron of European intercultural experimentation are not just a few Kathakali exercises or yogic techniques, but both the mind of the practitioner and, through her body, "the existential ground of culture and self" (Csordas 1990, 1994). Taking a lead from Csordas' scholarship on embodiment, we come to a richer understanding of the conflict when, instead of reading into the taboo of mistreating a book, we reference Sanjukta's existential experience of her own living body, and through her body, her experience of her culture and self. My insight from my lived experience of the Indian caste system suggests this incident is as much about her not wanting to kick and mistreat a book as it is about her relationship with her own body and the culture unconsciously encrypted on it, by which a foot stands condemned as impure, lesser/least in status as compared with the rest of her body and the body itself, lesser in status than the book.

My insight holds the pre-knowledge of the encrypted hierarchised body, an essential part of the Indian caste system, where the head and mouth are considered pure and sacred, belonging symbolically to the highest *brahmin* caste, the body with the chest and arms to the *raja/kshatriya*'s or warriors, the legs to the *vaisyas* or merchants and the foot the lowest to the *shudra*[6] or the servants, and with the untouchables or pariahs considered as dirt below the feet. Writing of the primordial super male *purusharth*'s body, noted historian and Indologist Arthur

---

6 I use the term *sudra/shudra* while acknowledging that the politically correct term is Dalit. I use it, not empirically, but conceptually and with reference to the caste-encrypted body in the context of 17th-century texts.

L. Basham quotes the Rig Veda: "The Brahman was his mouth, of both his arms was the Rajanya made. His thighs became the Vaisya, from his feet the Sudra was produced" (Basham 1989:24). Each individual body absorbs and is imprinted by this encryption. My own head is my highest part, my feet my lowest, untouchable. Significantly this caste-encrypted body exists as an absence. This is to state the obvious. Viscerally, no one feels any body part differently from another. No one experiences/senses their feet intrinsically of lesser import than their own hand. It is as culture that the encryption plays itself out, setting up the feet as the lowest part of the body hierarchy.

Within the Panigrahi–Barba incident, there are two social practices that this insight highlights. First, the taboo on kicking with one's foot a book, and second, the placing/perceiving of the untouchable as separate from the caste-hierarchised social body and placed even lower than the foot, as dirt beneath the foot. The common underlying principle between these two practices is the principle of untouchability (see Sadasivan 2000) framed by the rules and culture of the caste system that work on values of purity and impurity (Dumont 1970). This linking principle connects these two social practices to other practices that make up the Indian social habitat known as the caste system. Thus, the caste system and its practices of untouchability inform the act of Panigrahi's refusal to kick the book. Her own caste-encrypted body and its rules and principles, however, exist as an absence both to herself and to the other, to Barba. This encrypted embodied self and its principles and practices work not through Panigrahi's conscious will and control but as if automatically, unconsciously. Seen and understood through the tool of her body and its encryption, her embodied gestural display, her refusal to kick the book, is now located within the old social habitat of the Indian caste system. This culture exists as an embodied absence – the caste-encrypted body is absent from consciousness.

For example, the laws of body pollution which frame the hierarchy, with the *brahmin* on top being the most pure and the *shudra* at the bottom being the most impure (Dumont 1970), has another manifestation. The pure–impure binary is reflected by the left hand being the polluted hand and the right hand, the non-polluted. So, you eat your food with your right hand and use your left hand in the toilet. However, there is no visceral experiential difference in the feeling between one hand and another. Both hands feel the same to oneself. One hand does not intrinsically feel dirtier than the other. The encryption of the left- and right-hand differentiation exists as an absence. This caste-encrypted body is driven by structures and principles of which it is not consciously aware. These principles and practices work to place the body into the power structures of the social order and the caste system. These practices and principles then exist in the body as a "habitus" (Bourdieu 1990:52–65).

My interpretation of Bourdieu's "habitus" helps me engage with the logic of individual practices like feet touching and see how they make sense in the greater construct of the social world and power structures they inhabit. Within the Kathakali learning space, as observed and documented at the International Centre for Kathakali in New Delhi, this practice facilitates the inclusion of the learner into an empowered learning space. I harness ideas of both embodiment and habitus into the practical task of revealing my existence in both Kathakali practice, and the social world of the caste system.

In the present context, from a wider construction of the historical process of the representation of eastern, Asian, Indian arts through to a particular conflict between Barba and Panigrahi, we have moved to potentially a real moment of intercultural reality. Embodiment and habitus now become my tools to help gain an understanding of the real problem existing between Barba and the eastern master practitioner or *guru* Sanjukta Panigrahi. One aspect of the real problem is the dancer's body encrypted with the embodied culture of the Indian caste system that prevents her from obeying the director. Barba too, by not offering a solution (he could have found another way to do the scene which Varley does not suggest he did), returns a conflicting gesture, insisting she obey the needs of the situation while not offering an alternative. The potential for an ugly conflict emerges.

I highlight this conflict not to denigrate and devalue the intercultural exercise but to show the consequence of the real presence of the other. I would also like to clarify here my disinterest in Barba's motivations or his side of the story. I am interested in Panigrahi here, and I am using her story as revealed through the available literature to come to a conceptual understanding of a conflict within an intercultural exercise and through it reflect on her embodiment, her embodied experience of her culture and self. Going further, in this conflict the practitioner's body is not just the existential ground for culture and self, but through its potential for embodied gestures, through its performativity, a real, live and potentially conflicting presence for the other. It is this embodied gesture that I am interested in examining. In the present intercultural exercise between Barba and Panigrahi, a gestural display of embodied aggression, a refusal by one to obey the instructions of the other to kick the book, reveals two separate cultures at play. This conflict becomes even more interesting when you frame the existence of the cultural encryption on Panigrahi's body as an absence. Panigrahi is not consciously aware of her foot's lower status. She does not perceive or experience her foot as untouchable or lesser in status than the rest of her body. Her refusal to kick the book is not because she actively feels her foot lesser in status than any other part of her body (for example, her hand); she would have been willing of course to touch the book with her hand. Her body feels to her as one, and the same. What she is conscious of is the social practice of not mistreating the higher status book. It is about the book, not the foot. The experience of the lower status foot is absent. The caste-encrypted socially hierarchised body exists as an absence.

In addition to this particular conflict between Sanjukta and Barba, there is another foot-centred moment in their relationship that is of interest here. As a mirror image to the previous conflict, this time Sanjukta's gesture is submissive and conciliatory and Barba's passive, conflicted but not conflicting. Here is Varley once again, reporting as if from the scene of a crime:

In 1986, Sanjukta came to Holstebro with Kelucharan Mahapatra. During this ISTA session, I saw how Odissi dance could become like a Neapolitan popular play when Sanjukta did not interpret it. The pupil seemed more mysterious and fascinating to me than the master. It was also the first time I saw Sankjukta bend down to kiss Eugenio's feet, as a form of respect to greet a master. Eugenio, embarrassed, tried not to submit to this ceremony. In the same way that she followed all the formalities towards her Guruji, Sanjukta was adamant.

(1998:249–273)

The socially informed bodies of both Panigrahi and Barba, with their separate tastes and distastes, compulsions and embarrassments, with all their senses are at work now. In the presence of her own Indian *guru*, Sanjukta is displaying her social sense of devotion, a sense of respect for her European *guru*. By kissing his foot, the body of the European *guru* too is now hierarchised and encrypted with Indian culture. He is now conceptually (and not empirically) a *brahmin*, and a respected teacher. Sanjukta is, through this gesture of devotion, marking and branding their embodied relationship as teacher and student. Through the practice of foot kissing, between Barba and Panigrahi there is now a shared habitat. For the moment, it is India in Europe. Despite Barba's embarrassment, there is complete sense here driven by a shared habitus.

Unlike Barba, who could not escape despite what Varley describes as his embarrassment, I was able to refuse and stop Helen from touching my feet. I was conscious of not wanting to be turned into an exotic other for her (I term her gesture exotic as she wanted to accord me a status by a practice whose logic she was not aware of or not really concerned by). Even at the start of the relationship when Helen, habituated by her Butoh-led Japanese experience of calling her teacher *sensei*, asked what a traditional Indian teacher was called and if I would be happy with her calling me that, I had refused. I had insisted she call me Arjun. I wanted to stay real, as myself. While she was not aware of the principles that drove the practice of feet touching, I certainly was. My refusal was as much about a social practice that reflected for me the inequity of the caste and social hierarchy in India as it was a need to be in control of, and to distance myself from, an exotic identity on offer in this social habitat into which Helen was, by playing her part, offering to locate me as a *guru*, a teacher worthy of his feet being touched! My refusal to be deemed exotic, even as a well-respected other, compelled me to search for an alternative that was driven by principles, consciously crafted and acceptable to me.

Conclusion

In this chapter I examine the literature of two seminal practitioners, academics and researchers engaging with the processes of Kathakali actor training – the work of Phillip Zarrrilli and Eugenio Barba. I locate their representation of eastern arts and Kathakali within my needs of engaging with and creating a real actor-training programme in Australia. I take forward in this chapter my central argument of the need for the centrality of the Kathakali *guru* or teacher's presence in a sociopsychophysical intercultural actor-training programme. This presence of the body of the Kathakali teacher moves the exotic engagement towards the real, and I use real conflicts between Eugenio Barba and Sanjukta Panigrahi to theorise and understand the embodied, real presence, in a particularly influential European practice, of the eastern other. This presence of the Indian dance *guru* then includes as an absence her caste-encrypted body. By this embodied presence and absence, I moved this chapter from a making exotic of the other, to the potentiality of a real engagement with the other.

4   Teaching multiple bodies in Australia

After my introductory workshops discussed briefly in the previous chapter a number of participants agreed to continue working in the group workshop mode. From August 2014 to October 2014, for three months, I worked with a group of Australian performing artists from a range of practices, including Butoh, BodyWeather, ballet, Odissi dance, stage and television/cinema acting. We worked for one hour a week at a hired studio in Melbourne. The learning process throughout this entire engagement followed the traditional methodology established, which was to demonstrate for the participants the action to be performed, and then ask them to mirror and perform it. As stated earlier, I was not going to engage in any detailed discussion through this process. The only method on offer was my repeating the action demonstrated as often as they asked for it.

The mirror neuron system

To teach Kathakali in Australia, I needed to find at the first instance an appropriate language and representation. Readings in neuroscience literature offered a contemporary language to present the Kathakali work. In my workshops, I had to speak in English, and ask learners to observe me, to watch me carefully, to imitate me. To observe is to do in Kathakali. Kathakali learning involves a sustained observation, over many years, by a learner of a *guru*. The value of this sustained observation may be validated by developments in our understanding of the way the brain works. Recent excitement in the field of neuroscience suggests that there exists a mirror mechanism in the human brain supporting the "intersubjectivity" involved, as happens in the intimacy of social interactions wherein a mirroring takes place, one parallel to that of the mirroring of a teacher's actions by a student. This "intersubjectivity" generated by the mirroring mechanism mediates by integrating the act of observing with the act of doing; as Gallese observes, "[m]irror neurons are premotor neurons that fire both when an action is executed and when it is observed being performed by someone else" (2009:520).

This integration, through a precise imitation of the act of observing and doing, is the core methodology of the "Kathakali mirroring" process. Gallese and Sinigaglia set out the working of the mirroring mechanism in greater detail:

this mechanism in the human brain, given the present state of knowledge, maps the sensory representation of the action, emotion or sensation of another onto the perceiver's own motor, viscera-motor or somatosensory representation of that action, emotion or sensation. This mapping enables one to perceive the action, emotion or sensation of another as if she were performing that action or experiencing that emotion or sensation herself.

(2011:512)

What is significant here about the activation of the mirror neuron system is not that a motor neuron (one that moves the body) fires when an action is performed, and another visual neuron (one that helps observation) fires when that same action is observed. It is that the same motor neuron fires, for instance, when the monkey grasps a peanut as when the monkey observes another monkey grasping a peanut. These neurons were called mirror neurons because it was as if the monkey was watching her own actions reflected by a mirror when watching someone else performing the action. It is as though this neuron is adopting the other person's point of view, performing a virtual reality simulation of the other person's action.

In the context of Kathakali learning and performance, what may be inferred here is that the same motor neuron that fires when a teacher's action is observed by the learner is the motor neuron that fires when the same observed action is performed. The power for the Kathakali learner/performer comes from the integrated process by which a motor neuron fires twice, as it were, firing once while observing the dramatic action being taught and firing again when enacting that action. This process is facilitated by an act of empathy. This empathy works itself out connecting two bodies separated at the surface of, and by their human skin. This empathy is heightened when the action observed is precisely imitated. Through that precise enactment the teacher and the learner experience a communion, a oneness, losing their sense of separation. This communion I suggest from experience is an aesthetic pleasure. The Kathakali learner's body then communes with the teacher in the learning space, and, with the audience in the performance space, creating conditions for an experience of aesthetic pleasure or *rasa* for both performer and audience.

The human skin and the act of empathy

In a TED talk (2009), neuroscientist Dr V.S. Ramachandran, reflecting on what makes for two individuals experiencing themselves as separate from each other, suggests that it is the sensitivity of their skin that effects a feeling of separation. A sense of touch received through the human skin, as perceived by the human brain, furthers the ownership of a separate experience. Ramachandran's ideas about the way the brain functions are central to the argument being made here. A TED talk by him is used as a reference, both for the knowledge it contains as well as the performative act, the stepping out by the scientist into the performance space, arguing for and stating a new understanding of the way brain activity informs culture, an understanding that makes more complex the act of imitation.

As a teacher of Kathakali in Australia, my articulation in English of an appropriate representation to validate its imitative teaching methodology is a similar act of performance. I needed to communicate and convince the learner by using an appropriate language. To have the learner's attention and empathy I needed to find the right words and language. Within the Kathakali actor-training space, I needed to activate what Ramachandran, mooting human connectivity, playfully calls "Gandhi Neurons":

> So, I call them Gandhi Neurons, or empathy neurons. And this is not in some abstract metaphorical sense. All that's separating you from him, from the other person, is your skin. Remove the skin, you experience that person's touch in your mind. You've dissolved the barrier between you and other human beings. And this, of course, is the basis of much of Eastern philosophy, and that there is no real independent self, aloof from other human beings, inspecting the world, inspecting other people. You are, in fact, connected not just via Facebook and Internet; you're actually quite literally connected by your neurons.
>
> (TED talk 2009)

To make sense of Ramachandran's hypothesis in the present context, I turn to Kathakali's body massaging practices. In Kathakali's body preparation practices, one element of what Drew Leder defines as the "surface body," the skin, and its ecstatic opening out to the world, is enhanced through the process of daily oil massage called *uzhicil*. The body is massaged for long stretches of time, not just for days but for months, day after day after day.

Why does the actor-training process require such intensive massage? One explanation references the earlier elaborated idea of Leder's "disappearing body." The massage opens the young learner's skin and senses to the world, and by that very ecstasy makes the body comfortable with the state of absence, with the body's disappearance. After a month or more of the oil massage, the sense of being relaxed, free, of being bodiless, airy, etc., are all part of that greater sense of embodied disappearance. The oil massage serves not just the body's flexibility and relaxation but also helps develop that inner subjective state of calm, of absence, of a comfort with the body's disappearance. This subjective relaxation and comfort facilitate the embodiment of the *bhava* or the embodied emotional state. When the performer generates and fills his body with the specific embodied emotional state, the subjective body is ready to receive the *bhava* and the performer, too, gets to be comfortable with this inner possessed state. By this process, Kathakali training habituates the performer to the phenomenology of the body's disappearance allowing for the body's possession by the emotional state or *bhava*.

The body's absence and disappearance also facilitate its communion with the other, the body of the teacher. The learner's internal body image, freed of its sense of its limitation by an intense massage of its outer surface, its skin, is easily morphed into and absorbed as it were into the body image of the teacher. Through a sustained social interaction, the two bodies feel as one. Yet they maintain their separateness. As Ramachandran suggests, it is the skin that separates, facilitating identification. The well-oiled and well-trained body of the Kathakali learner, observing the teacher's demonstration, experiences the teacher's action, the Kathakali form, its objective and subjective condition, as if it were his own. This state of deep empathy is heightened by the precise observation and imitation of the action observed. This process of precise observation and imitation facilitates a communion between the learner and the teacher. The loss of ego, of a sense of separateness, then facilitates the magic of mirroring the master.

The imitative methodology in group work

I stand before a group of Kathakali learners in a small studio called "The Yellow Room" at the Abbotsford Convent in Melbourne. I have hired the studio for an hour-and-a-half every Friday of the month. I had advertised these classes as an introduction to Kathakali actor training. I've had a great response and find eight enthusiastic learners waiting for me on the first day. The room has a window looking out westward, and the evening sun is flooding into the room. There is a large mirror on one wall which I had hoped to keep to one side of us, but have to adjust myself because of the sunlight, and stand in front of it, with the learners facing me and facing the mirror. There are different ages, ethnicities, body shapes and genders facing me. For issues of privacy, letters of the alphabet represent each of them.

A is a short, strong, powerfully built middle-aged woman. B is an edgy, nervous, slim-bodied young woman. C is a young man, shy of his physical presence. D is a tall, large well-built middle-aged woman. E is a neatly framed, slim-boned, contained and reserved young woman. F is a strong-bodied, powerfully built young man. G, is a thin, tall, wiry and unsure-on-his-feet middle-aged man. H is a tall, well-controlled, precise young man with a very wide arm-spread, making him look like an albatross in mid-flight!

I begin the actor-training session with the folded hand salutation, then the three steps backwards and into the basic pose. This takes a lot of time. It is surprising to see how slow they are in co-ordinating their left and right hands as well as their hands with their feet. This lack of co-ordination becomes even more apparent when we attempt two-handed gestures, with each hand illustrating a different gesture.

E, who is an Odissi performer, another form of Indian dance with its own hand gestural language, is quick to adopt Kathakali's language of gestures. D too over time finds a good rhythm but the rest of the group find it very difficult. G, who is the oldest in the group, interestingly finds gestures that bring the tip of the forefinger and the tip of the thumb together, almost impossible to remember and master.

After attempting the folded hand greeting, I move to working steps backwards to rhythm. The steps in rhythm take more than one session to master. Stepping backwards seems more difficult than stepping forward. It is clear in doing this simple step to rhythm that these bodies in front of me have not previously moved to a formal rhythm such as Kathakali's *taalam*. Taking steps backwards in rhythm proves difficult and is time consuming. I find that while I am showing one learner the steps, the others are trying to find their own way into it. For example H has changed the *ti ti tai* chant to a one, and a two, and a three. The sound of *tai* pronounced with an elongated *taieeeee* can be stretched and allows for a little more space before the next beat. The count of three is more precise and limiting. I do not want them to count in numbers. I want them to observe and imitate me; this means I need to demonstrate it eight different times, once for each of them, and then work with each of them to get the chant and the step in sync. It proves quite exhausting and we barely have time to work at the basic pose.

I am keen and committed to working the basic pose every day. On the first day, I realise each individual requires a lot of attention. For the basic pose, each body has a different way of lowering itself and at the same time holding itself up. For example, G goes into a deep low square squat with his knees open wider than necessary. This results in his upper body and chest jutting forward almost aggressively and his arms stretching out, very square to the body. I need him to make his arms more rounded and release and relax into each element of the basic posture. I sense his body in two parts with him holding together the upper part far too tightly. This makes it feel as if he is disconnected to the lower part. Even though his posture is low and square, he doesn't feel grounded. E has great form and stands low and grounded on the one hand, and relaxed and free in the upper body on the other. However, her foot, used to the Odissi dance form, opens out at an angle. For Kathakali, I need to have it straight. This is a difficult choice. E has come to Kathakali to work at *abhinaya,* or the expressive enactment, including her facial and emotional expression. How could I teach her Kathakali *abhinaya* without affecting and changing her Odissi form? I am unsure of the answer. H has an excellent basic pose with wonderfully rounded arms. However, I sense he is holding his breath, and this makes for a lot of tension in the body. A is very committed to going low, but I have to watch very carefully so that she does not suffer pain in the knee joints. With everyone I sense a difference for the length of time each can and needs to stay down. This is a critical skill for the Kathakali teacher. To lower the learner into the basic posture, to watch them carefully as they stay down and at the right moment, to release and return them back to the upright. Each day, this needs to be done very carefully and the time increased slowly. Each individual has a different sense of being grounded and each has to be worked at separately. I find this critical element of grounding the learner very difficult to achieve with eight bodies present in front of me. Each archetypical gesture needs individual attention best served not by the group mode but by the one-on-one site of actor training.

Over the next three months, on every Friday, I work with the group. The numbers ebb and flow as the participants make their choices. In the group phase, often left on their own while I work on an individual, I notice participants working out their individual solutions to some of the difficulties they are facing. Difficulties range from performing fluently the two-handed *mudras* or hand gestures, to getting the danced choreography right. I notice they are doing two things, taking personal ownership of their problems as well as creating their version of the solution. This further results in the creation of their own artificial version of the Kathakali form. Taking personal ownership of problems and finding their own individual solutions makes the learner work within their own psycho physicality/ psychophysicality, changing the sociopsychophysical nature of Kathakali learning wherein the social informs the learner through the embodied presence of the teacher. I notice that whenever D is not able to do an action, she tries to identify it, and see and own it as a problem, to be analysed and solved. She seems to be asking herself "why am I not getting it?," while simultaneously applying her mind in trying to solve it. I hear G too say something to the effect of, "my mind is not getting it, so let me just see, if I go with the rhythm, I might get it." My belief is that as long as the performer is not able to see clearly what the body is being asked to do, the problem remains. For the performer to be able to see the Kathakali form, she must observe without interruption and in as pure, uninterrupted and unself-conscious a way as possible. The moment the physical form is seen as a problem, the learner's attention moves to finding the solution and not to the observation of the action. This creates other versions of the solution, interpretations other than the one which emerges through sustained observation.

In group work, this methodology of asking for a sustained observation of demonstrated actions was not easy. Time and again, I found the learner/s introspecting in my presence. Often, I could see them not watching me, and even while seemingly observing, trying to work something out in their own minds and bodies. Repeatedly, I would have to remind them of my presence, to watch me, observe me. I would say "Don't look up trying to remember the gesture, I am here, showing it to you, observe my gesture." I could see D working out the moves in her own head, in her own coded language that she had created on her own. Her own inner dialogue was so loud that I could almost hear it. On my insistence, she shared it. She had given a name for every move with the logic of a waiter serving a meal. "Hand up flat, holding a serving dish, three steps towards the table, bend to place plate, leap back as if seeing an insect in the soup!" She had created her own internalised social language. In the group sessions, I was unable to bring her attention to my needs, to the needs of the Kathakali teacher.

It was only later, when working one-on-one, that I could negotiate and find a way for the learner to give me his/her full attention. In the one-on-one space, while the learner was constantly confronted by my presence, neither of us could escape each other. In the group space, the opposite was true. While I was attending to one, the others would turn inward, beginning to introspect, finding their own ways. I had to devise different strategies to draw their attention to my presence. I had to physically exaggerate some gestures or make a louder noise with the rhythm stick. For a long time, D had the habit of making a particular popping sound when getting a rhythm right. It was her way of announcing to herself that she had done the step right. I had to intervene to break that habit. I would stop teaching the moment I would hear the sound. It took a while for the message to sink in. The Kathakali learner has to be silent, watchful. Like a hunter warrior out on a hunt! G kept looking abstractedly into space, to remember gestures, and insisted he was a visual person and needed to refer to his visual memory, which was way up there somewhere. I was showing him the gestures and needed him to do them precisely till he was sure of them, not attempting an interpretation of the action, recalled from a memory space, but presenting a real version of what I was offering.

I found I had to ask the learners to stay within the grounded environment of our relationship. In common parlance, I needed the learner to stay in constant touch with me. At the same time, I had to attend to each of them individually, separately. This proved extremely difficult. It was easier to start talking and explaining things than to repeatedly demonstrate for them. I had to find persuasive and contemporary arguments to highlight the importance of a need to sustain observation. This brought up the question of the language I used to argue my case. How do you ask a contemporary western performer to observe an action and then to copy, imitate or mimic the observed action? How do I ask an Australian learner/actor/performer to observe my action and then copy, mimic, imitate me repeatedly, till it is perfected? Mimic your way to become perfect impersonators! I noticed the learners observe and receive an action and then move very quickly to owning and interpreting it. Living in Melbourne for the past five years, I have shared a culture where one individually owns and executes actions all day – from washing clothes and dishes, to shopping for and cooking food, to removing garbage. Here in Australia, all these are not social joint actions (as they are for me in India) but singular, individualistic acts. I had to find a new language and culture to adapt to the needs of both, the traditional Kathakali training methodology, as well as the Australian learner. From this, for example, emerged the need to define the imitative learning process as an act of Kathakali "mirroring," referencing not the inversion of an image in the mirror but the functional value of mirror neurons within the mirror neuron system in the human brain. This reframing of the act of imitation and placing it within the contemporary language and culture helped justify the repeated requests to observe and then perform and mirror my actions.

Through teaching groups of performers and attending to their individual needs I realised all performers, each in their own ways, have special needs. For example, G had a habit of pursing his lips each time he committed to an action. This was a personal nervous habit no one else had ever noticed. In Kathakali, the face, including the lips, is made up into a precise facial form. A pursing of lips would destroy the form. The precision of the form needed him to break his habit of pursing his lips. This required me to intervene into his personal space and constantly remind him of his habit each time he pursed his lips. In a group session, this was embarrassing. Later, the trust, intimacy and privacy of one-on-one work allowed this significant intervention. Over time, G let go of his habit, experiencing a deeper relaxation as a consequence.

While dancing, E was getting breathless very easily. She seemed to be struggling with body movements, which she was sure of and had mastered, to the traditional music. She had always listened to the traditional music while attempting the formal dance. Perhaps she needed to find a new way to listen to the traditional music – by free dancing to it. She responded to the free dance session in the following way:

So, when I was dancing freely to traditional music it felt like I was actually listening to the music and not worrying about what my body was doing as much as I would usually. I heard and experienced flows of rhythm that I normally wouldn't whilst dancing the traditional form. There was a freedom in breaking out of the form and it felt a little rebellious too!

(Personal email to author dated 4 April, 2016)

This was a great response and I felt emboldened to include it for other learners, free dancing to traditional music, as a means not for performance but to help them deepen their connection to the music. However, these solutions within the group work began to take the teaching away from its core principle of demonstrating, observing and imitating. While being more creative, I found myself compromising on the core research exercise which was to renegotiate the basic exercise of observe, imitate and repeat. As a teacher, I was beginning to invent exercises to help solve individual learners' problems. This was moving me away from the objective of the research exercise. I needed to draw the participants back to the research objectives, not solve actor-training problems as if we had a show to perform. I needed to work at the act of imitation and move the learners to trusting the creativity within the imitative process.

As Hallam and Ingold point out:

Copying or imitation is not the simple, mechanical process of replication that it is often taken to be, of running duplicates from a template, but entails a complex and ongoing alignment of observation of the model with action in the world.

(2007:5)

Working with the above articulated assurance, the learners needed to trust in this process of observation, imitation and mirroring. They needed to be convinced of the many innovations within the imitative methodology itself, elaborated upon here by Dalidowicz (2015):

Although less obvious, and harder to translate to pen and paper, instruction and interventions in dance come in other ways, from the subtle movements, emotive gestures, and expressions of the teacher, to more obvious methods like slowing segments down, emphasizing critical features, parsing choreography into manageable sections, or repeating isolated movements. The basic task of mimicry is, in fact, a product of interventions, based on the teacher's pre-understanding of basic problems and difficulties, made in response to the student's shifting abilities.

(2015:841)

Dalidowicz's observations validate the value of the imitative process supporting a master practitioner's effort to make the learner imitate more precisely. This trust in the imitative process is central to traditional pedagogy.

A sign that I was not taking on the role of the traditional teacher in the group sessions was my not taking up the central seated position of the teacher. Instead of the seated, dominant position, I would stand and teach, often at the side or even behind the group. Theoretically, in my head, I had framed the group phase as an "intracultural" (Bharucha 2000) exercise between fellow Melbournians of differing ethnicities, and consequently was attempting to create a more democratic exercise of my power as a teacher. An "intercultural" exercise perhaps would have required a more definitive stamp of the leading culture. My avoidance of the role of a central authority was a conscious choice and needs some explanation in the context of ideas emerging from the "intracultural" exercise.

The intracultural exercise

In negotiating the creative problems emerging from a "collision of cultures," Rustom Bharucha (2000) suggests working with the alternative concept of the intracultural as different from the intercultural. In an intercultural exercise, Bharucha suggests that the two cultures, separated in space and time, move towards common ground, a universal middle, a neutral space. This neutral space however is white, patriarchal and male in its primary dominant narrative. We saw this earlier in the conflict between Barba and Panigrahi wherein it was Barba's values that were driving the intercultural exercise, creating situations of conflict for Panigrahi. In the intracultural exercise, Bharucha frames a more equal negotiation of cultures, existing within a region, with an acknowledgement of each participating culture, and without a search for a universal common ground. For a director leading the intracultural exercise, he suggests that "to work with the acknowledgement of 'imperfect knowledge' could be the surest way of securing the trust of one's collaborators" (70). By standing to one side of the group or standing behind the group and not right at the centre, I was attempting to live out this idea of the leader with "imperfect knowledge." The knowledge that was being sought was not with me alone, but somewhere in between us, between the learners and me. By not sitting at the centre and making the group work at repeating my actions perfectly and instead innovating and inventing exercises, I was losing the core traditional methodology of making the learner observe and imitate actions perfected by the master.

This choice was reflected in a lack of clear directive of how to start and end a session. No formality had been established and participants were free to come in and leave. While staying away from using the feet touching ritual, the participants still needed a formal entry, in and out of the workshop. The work itself was formal and embodied. A mere "hi," "hello" or a "good bye" and a handshake felt inadequate for the work which was indeed a formal embodied exercise. I realised that this formality needed to be respected, followed. The formal practice itself seemed to be demanding a formal greeting. While refusing to go with the traditional feet touching exercise I felt compelled to reinvent one. The inadequacies of the "intracultural" exercise for research into Kathakali actor training then set the ground for a more rigorous examination of the traditional methodology including the one-on-one mode of training as evidenced by the work in the following chapter.

5 Working one-on-one with Helen Smith and Peter Fraser

This chapter documents the teaching of two Australian performers, Helen Smith and Peter Fraser, working at the one-on-one site of Kathakali actor training. At this sociopsychophysical site of one-on-one actor training, the psychophysicality of the learner mirrors the psychophysicality of the master practitioner. This mirroring is experienced as an embodied communion between teacher and learner. This communion lays the ground for an experience of aesthetic pleasure or *rasa*. In this chapter I document the journey to this transfer of *rasa*, arguing "it" as the central offering in an intercultural exercise like the teaching of an eastern art Kathakali in Australia. Using the convention of a "diary documentary" technique of on-site reportage, I share the practice-led work, as well as theorise around the question of the performer's pleasure or *rasa*.

Helen, Peter and I: working as a threesome

My work with Helen and Peter went through two stages over the 22 months it lasted (a period which includes the first 3 months of group work). Initially, we worked as a threesome before moving into the one-on-one space. This working together took place in Helen's home in the city. A small front room was enough to host three performers. Helen's home is an hour-and-a-half journey from my home in Gisborne, the first country town out of Melbourne. Afraid of city traffic and parking issues, I chose to drive down 20 minutes to a nearby town to catch the city metro. In the city I had to change metro lines to get to where Helen lived, a journey that required 90 minutes of travel in each direction. Peter lived near Helen's home. Helen and Peter had worked together before and were happy to form a pair of learners. While Peter seemed willing to undertake one-on-one work, Helen initially seemed a little reluctant, and was happier working in a group.

This initial plan had me spending a total of three hours travelling and often arriving to teach, a little tired and rattled by the journey. This limited my energy and I found our sessions restricted to an hour-and-a-half due to my getting tired by both the journey and the session being physically demanding with my need to demonstrate the actions repeatedly. Three months later, when we started to work one-on-one in my home, I found two significant differences. First, I could be still, calm and relaxed before starting the session. Second, Helen and Peter, working separately and one-on-one by now, both had cars and found they could drive to my home in 40 minutes and were less tired than I was by my travel. By this shift in work location, we were able to work for four/five hours at a time. The work itself, through an availability of time, felt deeper and richer. It also felt meaningful that the learner was moving towards a still/stable teacher. This formality felt right for an embodied practice like Kathakali wherein the teacher must often work as hard as the learner. However, initially I respected Helen's need to work in her own space. I later interviewed and recorded her feelings about her resistance to moving out of this space and into the one-on-one space:

Arjun: So, we began as a group with the workshop if you remember and then we went solo one-on-one. How would you have felt if we had carried on the entire process as a group? What was your reaction on the move?

Helen: Personally, I would have liked it, I like group work and it suits my mode of learning and that comes from prior experience. I learnt dance as a child in a group class and I worked in an ensemble theatre company where we trained and worked together. I really love that because I don't feel singled out like I do on my own and it's like what you said about hearing other people's responses. I enjoy working with other people and seeing how they react to the work and it helps me, inspires me to watch other students struggling, and helps me to understand my own struggle more, because the teacher being the role model is already exemplary but other students in the class are like me, struggling, and we can work it out together. So, I definitely prefer being in a group but I understand, I accepted your reasons for going in that direction, it was also rewarding.

The interview with Helen from which this excerpt was taken was recorded at the end of the 22 months of working together and reflects the complications of working one-on-one. As Helen suggests, not all learners are keen to work one-on-one. While respecting and understanding Helen's reluctance for one-on-one work, I was happy and appreciative of her trust in the process, and her willingness to engage with the one-on-one work. As she indicates at the end of the excerpt, she was a willing participant. This willingness was important for the research, as indeed was the voluntary nature of the exercise. Peter too was willing, and the one-on-one work began for me in earnest when Helen and Peter starting coming to my home in Gisborne.

Working one-on-one: an informal "daily" start to the work

The Kathakali training work begins with their coming, one at a time, to my home in the country town of Gisborne, where at my doorstep they have to take off their shoes. I have a chair waiting for them at the door, for them to sit. It takes a while for Peter, who wears very complicated laced up shoes, to change to easier slip-ons. His left foot is fragile, painful at times, and he is protective of it. I have a cup of tea ready for them, or at times, make them a cup of tea even while they are settling and relaxing after their drive. I enjoy having them standing around watching me make tea. We spend ten minutes, or so, sitting around the table relaxing and talking, conversing about our lives. My wife Monica joins in and sets off a discussion about dance. She is an Odissi dancer, an older form of classical Indian dance from the Northern Indian state of Odissa. These 10 or 15 minutes spent are precious for their ordinariness. Our "daily" bodies, sitting, standing, lounging ordinarily. Our embodied voices touching each other. Washing up the tea utensils, we move to the studio.

In the one-on-one session, I attempt to work with the clarity and authority of a traditional teacher. In what can be framed as the Kathakali mirror box I am the well arm, the learner the phantom limb suggesting the pain involved for the learner. However, while I am attempting to play a traditional teacher, these are not traditional students. With Helen and Peter, and in respect of western traditions and habits of learning, the training sessions keep getting interrupted by their need to take down notes, and to ask questions. I am unsure and under-confident of enforcing my own rules of engagement. I feel obliged to let them participate in and direct the form of the work.

On being asked about his motivation for participating in the research exercise, Peter had expressed his desire to create a work with Kathakali and Shakespeare in the future. In an email, he had spelt out his attraction for what he believed was the kind of theatre Kathakali represented:

> I am not so interested in personal (self) expression and psychological narratives. I am most attracted to and moved by performance that does something like "resonating on the spot" – with a sense of being or presence or becoming. And of something human but larger or more universal than the individual human. Or something that is reached by means of gesture and state of the body.

Peter also had thoughts, though in the very early stages, of what he might do with the Kathakali work in the future:

> As to how I might "use" this. I am not sure. I do have a plan to work on a two-person version of Macbeth – perhaps focussing on grotesque elements (influenced by Ubu Roi) and using extravagant costume etc.
>
> (email to author dated 5 September, 2014)

Helen too had previously participated in a physical theatre performance of Macbeth[1] and was open to making creative explorations with Kathakali and Shakespeare. Both of them had just finished a Master's by Research and were keen note takers by habit of this previous research experience. They were both

---

1 *Macbeth: As Told by the Weird Sisters* by Zen Zen Zo Performer. Venue: City Hall Brisbane, VIII World Shakespeare Congress. Director: Steven Mitchell Wright. (Helen Smith c.v.)

open to working at a doctorate in the future. While not asking them to refrain from note taking or interrupting the work to ask questions, for my own part, I kept to the traditional method of not entering into a lengthy discussion. I tried to answer questions briefly while not getting into any detailed analysis, debate or discussion. I chose not to ever stop a session to take notes myself. Within the one-on-one site, I worked hard to not turn Helen and Peter into objects of my gaze/enquiry and continued trying to see them as Kathakali learners, and to encourage the concentrated, careful and sustained observation of the actions demonstrated by me. However, later, I would reflect on the process. This methodology of keeping the writing away from the training space maintained the authenticity of a pedagogy that has existed for centuries within a non-literate and oral tradition.

Susan L. Schwartz, in her study of the aesthetic pleasure of *rasa* (2002), offers a persuasive argument in support of treating these oral-based learning traditions differently from those that are literate:[2]

> The atmosphere in which teaching and learning took place was oral/aural/ kinesthetic. It is difficult to appreciate the power of this form of transmission fully, particularly from the standpoint of a primarily literate culture. If we are to understand the performing arts in India, however, this is one aspect that must be grasped. A distance occurs between the student and the knowledge to be gained when the mode of transmission is the written word. The physical distance between the eye and the page is symbolic of a greater distance between the learner and the learned. However, when the transmission is experienced physically, as sound enters into the body through the ears and movement is physically internalized, it is more active, more engaged, and it is immediate, that is, unmediated. Those who learn physically learn differently and experience their knowledge differently as well. It becomes ingested, becomes, like food, part of one's cell structure. When the guru *shows*, rather than *tells*, absorption by the student is of a different quality altogether.
>
> (5)

Schwartz's highlighting of the difference between the written and the "oral/aural/ kinesthetic" frames my methodology. The practice followed this methodology of the teacher showing rather than telling. The time to reflect on the work came later when writing about the sessions in the diary. On re-reading and analysing these reflections recorded in the diary, I found my writing suggested both, those sessions that I perceived as going well, and those points of breakdown and conflict in the relationship. It was in negotiating problems and conflicts that I had to work harder to understand the intercultural aspects of teaching Kathakali in Australia.

---

2 Diana Taylor too, in her forceful work *The Archive and the Repertoire: Performing Cultural Memory in the Americas*, argues for a recognition of this difference between the embodied and the literate. "For all of us the political implications of the project were clear. If performance did not transmit knowledge only the literate and powerful could claim social memory and identity" (2003:xvii).

Choosing to keep some traditional methods and practices while at the same time transforming others based on the needs of this new location was an important element of the work on hand.

The first problem awaiting resolution was finding an appropriate ritual to start the session, replacing the traditional touching of the teacher's feet. While rejecting the practice of the old social, in the new social I needed Helen and Peter to continue to make some form of respectful contact with my body. In our sessions together, we unsuccessfully tried various options. A handshake was too western. A folded hand greeting by both was eastern but a still a little like an exotic spiritual greeting. A hug was too intimate. A kiss on the cheek too alien to the culture of Kathakali. Starting only with the Kathakali *kumbatil* or formal greeting was another option, but that meant entering the training space without acknowledging the social space. For a while, we struggled with the replacement of the traditional hand to foot gesture.

It was in researching the way the body and the brain inform each other that I gained confidence in transforming the traditional practice into a new practice. The clue to creating the new practice came from reading Dr V.S. Ramachandran's work with phantom limb pain.

The mirror box

Dr V.S. Ramachandran created the mirror box to relieve patients of their phantom limb pain. For Dr Ramachandran, the first clue to understanding phantom limb pain came from the way different points on the body surface are mapped onto the surface of the brain. This map or representation, is in the form of a grossly misshapen little man, the so-called "Penfield Homunculus" (Ramachandran and Blakeslee 1998:25). This "sensory homunculus," as it is also now called, is a representation of the body surface on the outer layers of the brain. Its formation, in the shape of a short and oddly shaped man, has the lips and tongue grossly over-represented on the one hand and, significantly for our story, the hand and face placed right next to each other on the brain surface. This offers the potential of one space being neurologically available to the other neighbouring space.

At the heart of Kathakali learning and performance is an integration of hand gestures and facial expressions. This unity is at the core of the Kathakali performer's ability. Eugenio Barba describes the value to the craft of Kathakali storytelling, of this hand and face relationship.

> From this rule we can see that the face is the emotional counterpart of the story not by somebody else, but by the actor's own hands. In short, there is a double structure: the actor must resort simultaneously to two different sets of technique to express the two complementary aspects of a story, the narrative and the emotional. His hands "tell" the former, while his face expresses the latter.
>
> (1967:40)

The proximity between the face map and the hand map on the human brain is what first fired up my interest in the story of Ramachandran's mirror box.

From this fascinating piece of neuroscience around the sensory homunculus, Peter's, Helen's and my learning for the starting ritual of our training sessions was the following. The narrative and emotional significance of the hand and face connection to Kathakali performativity helped further the move away from a traditional hand and foot gesture to a hand and face gesture. In the new ritual devised by the three of us, the teacher puts out his folded hands, the learner bends slightly, not as much as he would have to touch the teacher's feet, and holds the teacher's hands in/with his hands, then leans forward and touches the right, then the left cheek with the teacher's cheeks. The process of writing this book helped me intellectually validate this new practice, as well as helped me argue the case with Helen and Peter for this new practice to replace the old one. This freedom to touch our faces was one available in the new social and I was happy to be able to use it, for my purpose of both acknowledging an intimacy and touchability within the one-on-one space in the new social, as well as expressing respect for each other's bodies. In the intercultural space available in the new social, the ability to make such adaptations was in itself a delight and pleasure.

Communing with Helen one-on-one: an episode from the author's "diary documentary"

To my home in Gisborne, Helen arrives sharp at 9 a.m. At the door while she takes off her shoes we have a little playful ritual greeting in German, "Wie Gehts … Zer Gut, und sie." Just fun. We sit down for a hot cup of tea. In talking with her, I find out she has just dropped a dear friend to the airport. I sense she is a little fragile by this farewell. We go into the studio and we both delight in the new hand and face greeting. She too is happy with it. She claps her hands in approval. I am now seated centrally in the room like a traditional teacher. She moves back, stands a few feet away from me, and does the formal Kathakali *kumbatil*. Even though Helen, through all her previous training, has a very strong sense of body grounding, when working to move her body to rhythm, she works with her mind, listening and trying to work out the rhythm in her mind, trying to connect the rhythm to her body, and when she does that, she tends to hop lightly with her steps. As her mind is working the rhythm out in her head, her body feels ungrounded. I decide to begin by working harder at helping her staying grounded, even as she works to move her body to Kathakali *taalam* or rhythm. To start the process, I make her stay in the basic pose for far longer than before. As she struggles to release herself out of the pose I keep indicating for her to stay lower. Helen is a fighter and struggles hard against her need to free herself. She stays low for a long time. I finally ask her to relax, reminding her that I need her to stay low through the entire session. For the next four hours, I keep indicating to her, not to bounce up, but stay low.

While staying low we begin to work at a little dance phrase that both Helen and Peter have had difficulty in mastering. It is a "full stop," that marks the end of more elaborate *kalashams* or choreographed danced steps. The *vaitari* or vocal chant accompanying the step goes

Dhit ta tat ta tim da ta di tai ta dhi ta dhiki ta tai.

The steps are "right foot in, right foot out, left foot in, left foot out, right foot forward, left foot forward, a left foot heel click and a simultaneous right foot kick forward, then a right foot heel click and a simultaneous left foot kick forward, then a quick right kick, right step, left step, closing with a final right step." This last phrase is to the rhythm of *dhi ki tat tai.*

I demonstrate this step repeatedly, endlessly it seems to me. This full stop takes Helen an inordinate length of time to master. The rhythm, which is cyclic, has a marker just before the final beat, to indicate the next cycle is coming up. The chant slows down after *dhi... ki...* and quickens with *tat tai.* This blurs its steady mathematical progression, complicating its imitation. The clicking of the heel and the simultaneous kicking of the other foot further makes this a complicated step for Helen.

While Helen wants to notate this step in her diary in ways similar to those I have just described, I want her to stay away from writing, to observe me instead, and try and mirror my action. I am happy to demonstrate it as many times as she requires me to. However, I observe her introspecting the moment she begins to mirror my action. Her head bends down and tilts sideways, and I can hear her mumbling, trying out the chant in her head. Her gaze is turned inward. I ask her to chant the *vaitari* aloud but find the chant has in itself become a challenge with the problem of mouthing alien sounds, and a difficult exercise on its own. When I suggest we leave this step for another day, Helen argues strongly for her need to perfect the step before she moves onto anything else. She wants to be left alone to work it out for herself. I need her to keep observing me and to keep trying to repeat the step. Her getting the step perfect is not important for me today. Her trying to get it perfect, and in the way I am asking her to do so, is more important. I realise I need to find a way of sharing my desperation. I tell her I feel like she is treating me like an artist's model, and while I stand there in front of her, she is working to make what looks to me like an impressionist painting of me. An impressionist painting acceptable to her but not to me. We are both upset by this image. I am aware she is emotionally fragile that morning. I could/should stop there and walk away but I sense it would be difficult for me to carry on. I have been trying to get through to her, to allow me to lead the action, for a while now. Helen continues to insist trying to work it out on her own, arguing she is a perfectionist and needs to work out for herself why she is not able to do a simple step. To find her own answer. As a final argument, I add to the image of the artist and the model, another image. One of a monkey and a scientist. I have felt like that each time Helen has taken an action and tried to analyse it while I waited, watching. Like a demonstrating monkey while the free and creative scientist/artist works things out. I suggest to her we both needed to be monkeys playing with, observing each other. I suggested a time for interpretation would come later, once she has communed enough with the form. This freedom to interpret at a mature stage of learning is available even in the traditional training method. However, at this stage, she needed to commune with me, and trust the process.

We were both moved by this image of difference. This was as hard for me to express as I could see it was for her to hear. I didn't doubt Helen's work ethic. I could have given in earlier, but I knew I had reached a limit. I had shared with her the research exercise of following the imitative methodology. I had presented my arguments. However, she was compelled by her own creative compulsions, training and culture.

We both ended the session there and chose instead to get the water boiling for another cup of tea. We both calmed down after talking of small inconsequential things. I was glad for this social space. By the time she left, we had a plan for the work ahead.

For the next session, she arrived, once again on time, to continue the work. Even in this, the very next session after the morning of our conflict, I found her far more observant and trusting of me, and the process. Our working relationship improved. I had been able to persuade her to follow my method not by the sheer weight of the traditional authority of the role I was executing but instead, through communicating my need, expressed to her verbally, to be seen as an equal. This critical negotiation was possible because right from the start of our relationship I had established a need for an equal relationship – Arjun to Helen – and not one of hierarchy that becomes established quickly through the feet touching practice. This equality helped sustain our social relationship, a critical element of the socio-psychophysical construct.

I felt very happy when, some months later at a performance that we did together, she revealed that this learning and performing of Kathakali had been one of the most pleasurable processes she had been involved with. We had moved from a potential brokenness that day, towards an experience of pleasure, towards *rasa*. Perhaps ideas and discussions of *rasa* between us had influenced her into thinking specifically about her own pleasure. Or perhaps this process was indeed pleasurable as she insisted. By making her follow my methodology, I was able to offer her what I had received from my own teacher, an ease of performing the hands, feet and facial gestures realised through the Kathakali form. This communion with one's own body parts and the ease of performing what at times is a complicated set of embodied gestures are, I suggest, a first stage of creating aesthetic pleasure.

This integrated body in communion with itself is driven by the rhythm or *talam* kept by the teacher. The teacher demonstrates the actions and emotions while keeping rhythm and singing the dramatic text. The communion with the teacher's actions, rhythm and "being" is then the second stage of aesthetic pleasure.

This is what the struggle with Helen was about, this communion with the teacher's body and rhythm, even for a little full stop. This communion begins even with a little phrase and then develops to negotiate complex choreography. The body of the Kathakali teacher holds within itself many stages of joy and aesthetic pleasure. A communion with that body starts from letting the teacher lead even for a little full stop. From this second stage, the bodies of the learner and teacher move to communing with the text, the singers and musicians in rehearsal. This is the third stage of aesthetic pleasure. The body of the performer, expressing on stage through all four forms of *abhinaya angika, satvik, aharya* and *vacika* and communing with the audience's body, especially of one who is knowledgeable of the aesthetic object on stage, is the fourth and final stage of aesthetic pleasure.

In traditional scholarship on the theory of *rasa*, the predominant interpretation of *rasa* engages with only the fourth stage. Here too it is the audience's experience that defines the meaning of *rasa*. The performer's body and its aesthetic pleasure are absent. In the following section, by examining the theory of *rasa*, the performer's body and its pleasure are added to the traditional idea of *rasa* as limited to an audience's appreciation and pleasure.

Theory of *rasa*

A theory of *rasa* or *a* taste of aesthetic pleasure, was first articulated in the *Natyashastra*, the second-century (AD) Sanskrit *Treatise* on drama. Over the centuries, one dominant interpretation of the theory separates *bhava*, the actor's embodiment of emotion, from *rasa*, the audience's taste or pleasure of the actor's embodiment. Zarrilli (2000a) validates this view:

> I am defining bhava as the state of being/doing embodied by the performer/ actor, as demanded by the dramatic context and interpreted within a particular lineage of acting.

> I am defining rasa as "flavor," or "taste," arising out of the act or practice of spectating which involves as complete as possible an engagement of the spectator in experiencing what the actor "brings forward" and embodies.
>
> (217)

However, *rasaabhinaya*, the common, traditional term used by actors in Kathakali for the training of *bhava*, sets up a contradiction suggesting that actors too are being prepared for *rasa*. Zarrilli (1984) documents this contradiction only to see it as erroneous, and reiterates the traditional scholarly separation of the performer's embodied emotion as *bhava*, and the audience's experience as *rasa*.

> It is interesting that for the Kathakali performer in common discussion and teaching, the exact differentiation between *bhava* (the performer's experienced and then projected emotion) and *rasa* (the audience's experience of the corresponding mode) noted above is not followed. Indeed, actors commonly refer to facial training and learning of the *bhavas* or emotional states as *rasaabhinaya*. Rasa, *which technically should only refer to the audience's experience of aesthetic delight*, and its savouring and experience of various emotions of the play, is commonly used to refer to the actor's projection of a character's emotions.
>
> (103, my italics)

Zarrilli references here and validates the traditional scholarly division between *rasa* and *bhava*.

Traditional scholarship suggests *rasa* is the audience's aesthetic pleasure and *bhava* the performer's embodied emotional state. Kathakali performers and embodied practitioners very commonly talk of their experience of training the embodied emotional states or *bhava*, not as *bhavaabhinaya* but as *rasaabhinaya*. *Rasaabhinaya* is a common, well-accepted term used in the wider field of Indian dance and drama training, as is another commonly used term, *navarasa*, to describe the nine embodied emotional states or *bhavas*. These terms suggest that performers too, by being trained for *rasaabhinaya* and *navarasa*, have a stake in the creation of aesthetic pleasure or *rasa*. If the audience experiences pleasure or *rasa*, does the performer too not feel an aesthetic pleasure? An evidence-based argument is presented in support of the performer's experience of *rasa*.

Evoor Rajendran Pillai, in an interview (2016), sets out the following point of view with respect to the performer's *rasa*:

> A performer must feel the aesthetic pleasure or *rasa* in his mind, of the performed *bhava*. For example if I show a character's *kopam* or anger without any experience of *rasa* or the pleasure of performing it, the audience will suspect that my head is full of anger. But it is not my personal feeling, the *rasa* I feel separates (clarifies) for the audience that it is not the performer's emotion but the character's emotion that both the performer and the audience are taking pleasure in.
>
> (Pillai 2016)

By this argument, *rasa* exists for both the audience *and* the performer.

In further support of this view is Sheldon Pollock's *A Rasa Reader* (2016), a comprehensive compilation of 1,500 years of critical writing on the theory of *rasa*. This period spans the time of the writing of the *Natayashastra*, from approximately the third century through to the eighteenth century. This expansive body of critical literature around the *rasa* theory attends to a few central questions. Where does emotion in dramatic literature first exist? In the poet, who first sees a deer dying shot by a hunter's arrow, empathises, and then creates a poem enriched by that empathy? Or does it reside with the reader who absorbs and experiences the aesthetic emotion in the poem? Or is it in the dramatic expression of that poem, in the characters of the hunter and the deer, and the creative artefact on the stage, or within the spectator who sees and experiences the artefact? These questions have plagued critics in India for a millennia-and-a-half. To frame the task before him, Pollock too uses the metaphor of a mirror, "a hall of mirrors."

> To watch ourselves watching something unreal, and willingly embracing that real unreality, no matter how sad or terrifying, is to enter into a fascinating hall of mirrors. Making sense of the reflection in this hall is what "aesthetics" in part is concerned to do. Although story telling in drama or poetry is a universal human practice, few people have meditated as deeply

and systematically on the questions it raises as thinkers in India, who over a period of 1500 years between the third and the eighteenth centuries, carried on an intense conversation about the emotional world of the story and its complex relationship to the world of the audience.

(1)

As suggested above, Pollock examines an extensive body of original, critical and literary texts in Sanskrit interpreting the theory of *rasa* and covering a period from the third century AD right up to the eighteenth century. His conclusions are significant for an interpretation of *rasa*. In the following section, a body of evidence is marshalled in support of the practitioner's experience of *rasa* with the argument presented that both *bhava* and *rasa* enrich the embodied creative artefact on stage. Pollock finds one interpretation (Krishnamoorthy 1968:45), with which, importantly, he is in agreement, that suggests that the theory of *rasa* in the *Natyashastra* was primarily concerned with the actor and the creative artefact on stage. The following conclusion arrived at through Pollock's research is significant here.

> A half-century ago a leading scholar of Indian aesthetics was correct to note and has been alone in noting that in the *Treatise* the words *rasa* and *bhava* [emotion] are used in connection with the actor and the artist and not in connection with the spectator, and that any 'historical approach' to these concepts must admit that they 'describe the aesthetic situation, the art object outside, more than the subjective state of the critic.' Although the scholar never worked out this historical approach, his intuition was correct, and the judgement about *rasa* fits with the overall objective of the *Treatise*: to provide guidance above all to actors. This objective is manifest in the work's repeated reference to how the components of drama, and the *rasas* in particular, are 'to be acted out,' and it was clear to the work's contemporary readers. 'The theory of drama' as Kalidasa puts it, 'is focused on performance.'
>
> (48–49)

This interpretation of the *Natyashastra* by the lone scholar Pollock identifies is different from the traditional view of *rasa* as belonging to the domain of the critic. The ancient drama treatise is, at the first instance, as argued for by the Indian scholar, and supported by Pollock, a guide for actors. *Rasa* and *bhava* are then terms first used for actor training. Pollock's estimation "his intuition was correct" leads the way for a reading of the Indian scholar Krishnamoorthy. This reading underlines *rasa* and *bhavas*' role in actor training and performance and not limited to the audience's experience. As Krishnamoorthy clarifies:

> What deserves our special attention here is the fact that the words *rasa* and *bhava* are used in connection with the actor and the artist, not in connection with the spectator. Bharata's *Natya-sastra*, if studied in this background, will show how nowhere are the words *rasa* and *bhava* confined to describe the spectator's exclusive experience. They are invariably used to refer to the

activity of the artists. In other words, a historical approach to the concept of *rasa* and *bhava* must admit that these two words describe the aesthetic situation, the art object outside, more than the subjective state of the critic.

(1979:5)

By this scholarly evidence, *rasaabhinaya*, the Kathakali practitioner's craft of training and taking pleasure in creating emotional states, or *bhavas*, is aligned with the theory of *rasa* as first articulated in the *Natyashastra*.

This book attends to this much neglected scholarly appreciation of the actor's *rasa* or the essence of the actor's subjective experience of the objective artefact on stage. Thus, drawing from my discussions with Pillai in August, 2016, is set out the following framework that underpins the operation of *rasa*. At the centre of the experience of *rasa* is the actor's embodiment of emotion. This embodiment, transformed into a creative object in performance, may then be perceived pleasurably by the "living body" of the performer both subjectively, from within, and objectively, as the art object. This subjective and objective perception holds true for the audience too. This aesthetic condition of the subjective and objective experience of aesthetic pleasure is then fertile ground for the tasting of *rasa*. This entire process may be seen in stages, set out below:

- The actor first creates, experiences, contains within the body and sustains for some duration a specific emotion. The actor's body is now transformed to a specific artistic object, a specific embodied emotion or *bhava*.
- The actor as subject experiences this object, this embodied emotion, this *bhava* even as through his craft, this *bhava* is sent forth, communicated, expressed and received by the audience (including the co-actors, singers and drummers on stage). Both the actor and the audience as subjects experience and take pleasure in the object, the aesthetic, artistic, embodied emotion or *bhava*. This is *rasa*.
- This communion of subjectivity between the audience/community and the actor, initiated by the same object, the specific *bhava* within the embodied artistic artefact on stage, and its self-aware conscious contemplation is *rasa*. The contemplation and experience of this single subjectivity by both the actor and audience is *rasa*.

This understanding of *bhava* and *rasa* in the context of joint action in a social situation is important because it brings the performer's living body into the scholarly discourse on *rasa*. An original construct of the sociopsychophysical representation of Kathakali aesthetics helps further frame an appreciation of the social along with the psychophysical.

Why has the subjective pleasure of the performer's body been absent from an aesthetic interpretation of *rasa*? The answer lies in an appreciation of the social weave, in the absence of the performer's body from this social weave, from scholarly representation. In a brahminical culture that has evolved over time and dominated this period of 1,500 years, text is the territory of the *brahmin* or upper caste.

To read, to use the mind, is to perform a purer, higher function than to labour with the body. The body exists within the social weave of the Hindu caste system as progressively *shudra* or lower in status and caste, both empirically and conceptually. Conceptually, anyone labouring with the body may be deemed a *shudra*. The *shudra* body or the actor's labouring body occupies the stage while progressively the *brahmin*'s appreciating mind spectates. It is this texture of the social weave that is seminal to an understanding of the sociopsychophysical aesthetics of Kathakali. In scholarly discourse, which is conceptually, if not empirically, *brahmin* in territory and practice, a separation is made between the pleasures of the *brahmin* patron and the *shudra* performer. A shift takes place in which the *brahmin*'s pleasure is present and that of the *shudra* is absent. A communion between performer and audience, which is the objective of the performance, is not polluted with the performer's pleasure and is purely the spectator's. Performer and audience cannot taste of the same food, of the same pleasure. The untouchable in the greater social weave, it is to be remembered, was not allowed to even draw water from the same well. Untouchability here is playing its part in isolating the audience's experience. In the following section, an understanding of this differentiation by caste is arrived at by appreciating the very social nature of Kathakali actor training and aesthetics.

Kathakali *rasaabhinaya* and the social nature of *bhava*

Kathakali *rasaabhinaya* is codified into the *navarasa* or nine codified "emotional states"/*bhavas* – i.e., *shringar* (desire), *raudra* (anger), *veer* (valour), *bhaya* (fear), *karuna* (grief), *hasya* (laughter), *vibhast* (disgust), *adhbhuta* (wonder) and *shantam* (peace). The preparation of a performer capable of embodying these *bhavas* is at the core of Kathakali training methodology.

> In Kathakali the emphasis is on the emotion or bhava, evoked at every moment in a performance. It is the finely nuanced aesthetic expression of the inner emotions that is of most importance in a Kathakali performance rather than the presentation of well-honed, even superb, technique.
>
> (Balakrishnan 2005:159)

The enactment of *bhavas* then, as this quote reconfirms, is right at the centre of Kathakali actor training. The following section sets out the social nature of *bhava*.

Zarrilli has *bhava* as an embodied "emotional state" (1984:103). In all available literature on Kathakali (Iyer 1955; Pandeya 1961; Jones and True 1970; Pitkow 1988; Balakrishnan 2005; Schechner 1988), *bhava* is described variously as emotion, sentiment or mood. Zarrilli, too, in his early work, writes: "The Kathakali actor's formal training includes nine basic *bhavas* or emotional states" (1984:103). Later, working through his psychophysical vision of actor training, Zarrilli works in the idea of *bhava* being a form of "being, doing" (Zarrilli 2000a:92; Zarrilli et al. 2013:57). This psychophysical, embodied state of being, doing is a departure from the conventional idea of *bhava* representing emotional states. Being, doing seems to lack emotion. In defending *bhava* as an emotional state, attention is being drawn to the social nature of an emotional state.

One reason for *bhava* being interpreted as a reductive psychophysical state of being, doing is Zarrilli's separation of an individual performer's personal feeling/state from *bhava*. *Bhavas* are not activated by personal feelings but are sociopsychophysical embodied emotional states. Zarrilli's being, doing does not address the social elements governing emotions, what emotion theorist James R. Averill identifies as the three principles by which emotions become organised into coherent systems of behaviour, i.e., "biological principle" (information encoded in the genes), "social principle" (rules and other cultural artefacts) and "psychological principle" (schemas or knowledge structures) (Averill 1990:391). By this understanding, *bhavas* serve as a potential communion within the social, between the singers, musicians, the teacher and the learner in rehearsal (*bhava*) and then between the singers, musicians, performers and the audience in performance (*rasa*). This shared social understanding of *bhava* is critical to the creation of the aesthetic pleasure or *rasa*. By this, *bhava* is not just about an individual performer's psychophysical state of being, doing but is more specifically about how that state of being, doing is shared. Zarrilli's descriptive of being, doing seems to uncouple the idea of the social, i.e., the family of singers, musicians, performers and audience, entirely from a representation of *bhava*. This social element of *bhava*, as a shared cultural artefact, brings an understanding, an emotional comfort, to everyone. By this, everyone can know and feel what that performer is being, doing.

First performed, as stated earlier, in the sixteenth/seventeenth centuries by the *nair* warrior caste and existing over the centuries within the Indian caste system, any representation of Kathakali is best served by an inclusion of the social. As Kathakali moved from the wooden masks used in earlier forms like Krishnattam, to the painted and masked face of the performer, it also moved from the divine archetype to the human archetype, from the stories of gods like Rama and Krishna to the epic heroes of the *Mahabharata*. These gods and epic characters have their place and roles within the social weave and religious culture of the Kathakali world. The Kathakali performer is trained to play out the sociopsychophysical gestures of epic human heroes and gods. I choose "gestures" over "actions" here, as I frame "actions" as that element of human behaviour that effects change in the environment while "gestures" do not.

In a traditional Kathakali performance, the audience knows the story. They know what the performer will do next. The "feeling" state generated in the body of the performer (and the character) is not a "motivation" to effect a surprising change in "behaviour" or in the action of the play. There are no surprises. The action is predictable. The characters too play out their pre-determined destinies, their fates. In the context of its predictable action, it becomes useful here to distinguish emotional from "motivational" antecedents. Motivational antecedents imply that the organism is preparing to or actually acting on the environment, whereas emotional antecedents imply only that internal processing, internal control mechanisms are in force (Scherer and Ekman (Eds) 1984:26–27). "Motivations" are "feelings" that translate into a change in the organism's behaviour or environment. Emotions, on the other hand, are "feelings" held within, contained within the skin of the emoting organism, effecting no outward change. In the context of Kathakali performativity, emotions are feelings generated in the body of the performer, through its sociopsychophysical gestures, held back, as it were, within the skin of the performer and existing as an emotional state or *bhava*.

Now, if in Pribram's theory emotion is held within the skin of the organism, then the question that begs asking is of its practical relevance to the emoting organism's behaviour. Pribram's theory answers this question with the suggestion that an organism's emotionally expressive behaviour plays its part in a socially communicative setting with its value dependent not on the emoting organism's behaviour but on the ability of other socially sensitive organisms to sense the meaning of its expressions.

> Thus, emotional expression does have a practical influence beyond the emoting organism, but only in a social communicative setting. In such a setting the practical influence is completely dependent on the ability of other socially receptive organisms to sense the meaning of the expression.
>
> (Scherer and Ekman (Eds) 1984:27)

In Kathakali, at the level of the performance, these socially sensitive organisms are the co-actors, singers, drummers and the audience, and their cultural sensitivity exists in their being able to read into the *bhava* or the contained "emotion" of the organism, i.e., the performer. *Bhava* is best described then as a self-contained embodied emotional state as it exists in a social situation.

To serve this social situation with a nuanced and coherent system of behaviour there exists the family of *bhavas*, including *sthayi*, *sanchari* and *satvik bhavas*. The *sthayi bhava* is the single, stable, permanent, enduring, base emotional state that underlies each scene or dialogue or sustained action. Overlaid on the *sthayi bhava* are more transient feelings and emotional states called the *sanchari bhava*. The *satvik bhava* is an involuntary expression of feeling or a spontaneous reflection or expression of the mind. In Kathakali, then, these families of emotional states get together, as it were, to create *rasa*. To delineate the logical steps of this process, Balakrishnan cites the *Natyashastra*.

In chapter Six Bharata Muni writes:

Vibhavaanubhaava sanchaari samyogaad rasa nishpathi

The emotion [bhava], with the combination of the cause [vibhava], reflection [anubhava] and the transitory mood [sanchari], creates an aesthetic experience or rasa.

(147)

These themes and variations of emotional states, as detailed above, are suggestive of emotion theorist Paul Ekman's concept of emotion families.

Each emotion is not a single affective state but a family of related states. Each member of an emotion family shares the eight characteristics I have described. These shared characteristics within a family differ between emotion families, distinguish one family from another (Ekman and Davidson 1994:19). This family of emotional states then serves the sociopsychophysical expression of *bhavas*. By contrast, Zarrilli's psychophysical representation of "being, doing" seems too singular, individual and reductive a term to represent the entire family, themes and variations and social world of *bhava*.

Bhava is experienced subjectively by a performer, not just as a state of being, doing but more accurately as a state of "knowing, feeling, being, doing." The first descriptive element of "knowing" is critical to an understanding of *bhava*. This knowing is shared by singer, teacher, performer and audience. This is how the emotionally expressive state of "knowing, feeling, being, doing" becomes a social, shared cultural artefact. The knowing is, further, a knowing of a feeling: there is a feeling behind the embodied emotional state that is recognisable and known to the performer. The audience too knows and feels this. This sharing with the audience of the knowing of the feeling behind the being, doing of the *bhava* is a pleasurable thing for the performer.

In addition to the audience's *rasa*, there is also the performer's pleasure of *bhava*, the pleasure in embodying an aesthetic emotional state. The existence of *rasa* is implicit in Balakrishnan's offering of his practitioner's embodied knowledge:

> This aesthetic emotion, which is developed by the creator, author *or performer* and is sustained for some duration, permits the receiver to forget his own individual identity and instead, experience oneness with the feelings and emotions of the works of art or the character of the literary text or the drama enacted in the stage. This aesthetic experience is Rasa.
>
> (128, my italics)

As Balakrishnan suggests, the performer, along with the author and creator, develops and takes pleasure or *rasa* in, and through his own creation. This book lays claim to a performer's right to experience pleasure in the crafting of a sustained aesthetic embodied emotional state.

The performer sublimates his individual self to become one with the character's emotional state while individuals in the audience step away from their personal selves to commune with the performer/character. The word for character (as in the list of characters of a play) in Sanskrit dramaturgy is *paatra* (vessel). The actor fills the vessel, the body of the character, his own body, with a specific aesthetic emotion. To begin this process, the actor's imagination is engaged and is sensitised to the story. The following is Balakrishnan's description of the process of evoking the performer's "inner emotional life":

> The initial seed for the evocation of emotion lies in the given circumstances of the story as detailed in the performance text or *attakatha*. These given

circumstances offer a clue to the cause or *vibhava* for the provocation of emotion. *Vibhava* is the cause which provokes the evocation of the *bhava*. It is of two types – *alambana*, that is, people, living creatures or objects that cause or evoke the *bhava*, and *uddheepna*, the circumstances, which help to enhance or inflame the *bhava*. *Anubhava* is the reaction or reflection of the *bhava* created by the onset of *vibhava*. "There are three avastas or stages in the process of the development of bhavas. They are beeja avasta (seed stage), ankruts avasta (sprout stage) and pallavita avasta (flourishing stage)."

(148)

This entire imaginative/creative process as detailed above leads to a significant event of subjective embodiment, the growth from an initial seed to a flowering of an embodied emotional state of "knowing, feeling, being, doing" and then the holding within the body of the *bhava* for a certain length of time. This is then crafted and directed towards, sent forth or offered to the audience, which then receives, absorbs, contemplates and experiences it as *rasa*.

Zarrilli describes this embodiment of the emotional state best when he adds to his idea of "being, doing" with the "being/feeling" and "emotion/bhava" binary. Here is his explanation of the difference between western naturalistic acting and Kathakali:

Part of the difference between the subtle "naturalistic" acting of the West and kathakali is that in kathakali, as in Japanese kabuki, this "filling" of the body is openly displayed and indulged, while in naturalism it is usually hidden and not obvious. The act of physicalization of the state of being/feeling of the character is intentionally "excessive" in the sense that the stage is the place to display openly the full or "pure" emotion/bhava, i.e., nothing need be held back to inflect or nuance its expression. These are, after all, gods, epic heroes, heroines and personalities at play on this cosmic stage, whose predicaments and responses to them are bound to be "larger" than everyday life.

(2000a:90)

This flamboyant display of emotion as recognised by Zarrilli here is a pleasure to perform. By defining the performer's pleasure this book separates the audience's experience from the performer's. In practice, the performer and the audience commune, i.e., the greater the recognition by the audience of a specific *bhava* or emotional state created by the performer, the greater is the performer's pleasure in expressing it. The sensitive and informed spectator or *rasik* communes with the performer, sharing the embodied experience. *Rasa* for the performer does not exist without an audience. It is social in nature. It emerges from "joint action" and a communion between the two, knowledgeable actor and audience.

The conflict with Helen, as described in the earlier section, in getting the little full stop correct through mirroring my actions, was a struggle towards an initiation into this sociopsychophysical aesthetic of communing with the master practitioner, and tasting *rasa*. This process moves through learning a brief choreographed full stop, all the way to performing scenes with archetypical gods and demons, epic heroes and demons, learning to perform their embodied gestures of aggression by communing with the master practitioner, and through the entire process tasting of *rasa*. In comparison with this very social, celebratory and outward aesthetic of Kathakali performance, the individual psychophysically absorbed western actor risks being introverted and playing without *rasa*. Coming from the sociopsychophysical tradition, my initial viewing of Helen and Peter's own creative expressions, as described in the next section, suggested to me a different aesthetic at work, one in which it felt as if the performers did not feel sure of where their pleasures lay – an aesthetic that was not necessarily seeking embodied pleasure, but that could perhaps benefit from Kathakali's sociopsychophysical offering of *rasa*.

Creative performances by Helen and Peter

Keeping their interest in Shakespeare in mind, and to see them working their own craft, right at the start of the one-on-one training, Helen and Peter were asked by me to use their own practices and create improvisations around archetypical moments from certain Shakespeare scenes with which they were familiar. On observing Helen and Peter performing, a lack of a certain outward socially directed openness was sensed. From a Kathakali practitioner's perspective, they seemed self-absorbed and not tasting pleasure or *rasa* in their own gestures. While Helen worked on the moment of Desdemona's death, Peter worked on what he framed as Iago's emotional state of jealousy, and the disgust at having to serve Othello. Their creations, using their own practices, were about four to five minutes long. They had chosen their own music and appropriate costuming. These were "work in progress" creations using costuming materials that were easily available. Throughout the process, we had no budget for any production work. They showed their creations to me in my working studio. There was no one else present. The work was video recorded and documented. This initial work was then used to reference and compare work done later, at the end of the training process

Helen's creation was her version of "Desdemona's journey to heaven." Though the rules of the exercise included not being pressured by any need to incorporate traditional Kathakali training in their creations, Helen had begun using certain Kathakali hand gestures, like the gesture of fear to reflect Desdemona's inner emotional state. Watching the work, an introverted, self-absorbed psychophysicality that seemed to fall short of displaying itself to the audience, shy of its social presence, was noted. This was a different aesthetic that seemed to be working with the fourth wall, unlike Kathakali, where there is no fourth wall. This same self-absorbed psychophysicality was reflected in Peter's contemporary creations exploring the theme of what would eventually be framed as "Iago the jealous dog." Both their works looked to me like experiments wherein the performers, even at the moment of performance, were more concentrated on solving a problem rather than sharing it with me, the audience. While this is no judgement on the artistic quality of their creations, which were indeed both very fine in their aesthetic textures, what struck me was the difference between Kathakali's bold outward sociopsychophysicality and their more inward, introverted, experimental psychophysicality. The imitative or mirroring work for the next 18 months was then directed towards drawing them out of their psychophysicality into Kathakali's sociopsychophysical. Through this process, fertile ground was being prepared for their bodies to experience aesthetic pleasure in performance.

Working with Peter Fraser

My second experience of one-on-one actor training with Peter Fraser furthered the challenge of taking a psychophysically trained performer into the sociopsychophysical space. While, on the one hand, Peter was mentally and physically extremely disciplined and capable, his will to mirror needed greater processing. For someone who had previously played, and brilliantly, a lizard locked up in a glass cage, as he had done in connection with his practice-led Master's thesis, the integration of hands, feet and facial expressions into an outwardly directed, socially meaningful dramatic gesture proved a more difficult task. To move him to take seriously the mirroring process, and through that enter into a communion with my ability to experience *rasa*, was a challenge. While consciously Peter worked to mirror my actions, perhaps unconsciously he was resisting. The consequence of this unconscious resistance, at times, was, what seemed to me, a shallow mimicry. This generalised mimicry from a physically disciplined performer was disconcerting for me, to say the least. We both had to find a way to get out of this generalisation, and be more precise with the mirroring process.

Right from the start of the group sessions, it was clear that Peter had a unique ability to run with an image and make something special of it. On an impulse, in a session, I had asked him to observe my demonstration of *rasaabhinaya* with each *bhava* being expressed through a bird or animal form, i.e., "desire like a peacock," "anger like a lion," "fear like a deer" and "disgust like a vulture," he was free to make of the form whatever came through to his imagination while keeping my demonstrated image in his mind. Peter responded by creating an amazing array of birds and animals with each embodiment expanding and contracting, breathing, shifting shape and size right before my eyes. We stayed with this kind of work for a couple of sessions and perhaps that was the cause of a certain derailment of the Kathakali work. While this interpretation worked well for what was primarily a visual image, i.e., of a vulture with my hands extended and my face contorted to show disgust, the moment rhythm and *taal* came in, his difficulties became apparent. For example, in a dance piece, in which there are series of complicated steps, Peter let go of the Kathakali form completely, and adopted a kind of salsa, hip-leading rhythm and style. This was his way of embodying and owning the complicated Kathakali rhythm. When I allowed Peter to find his own embodied way into the rhythm the work seemed to move much faster. He was picking up the actions quicker, helping build his confidence. However, it was at a terrible cost to the form. The work stopped looking and feeling like Kathakali, though he seemed to be enjoying himself a lot more. As he continued down this path, finding his own way into the gestures and actions, for my Kathakali-trained eye, it felt as if he was beginning to mimic the form through his quick, shallow, ungrounded imitation and adaptation of my movements. By this reduction of the form, one could understand clearly what mimicry looked and felt like, and how different it was from the mirroring being asked for. I realised each time I demonstrated an action that Peter was quickly absorbing a general view of my body image and running with an imitation of it. The pace we were working at was not allowing him to look at any action specifically, precisely, in depth, allowing him to integrate and co-ordinate the actions. The resultant mimicry upset me. When I tried to ask him to imitate specifically, for example, trying to get him to repeat the precise embodiment of a step, he would revert to his own methodology, asking specific questions, like which particular muscle was involved, or was the right hand leading over the left, or how many inches was the heel lifted off the ground, or was the weight resting on the balls of the feet. I had resisted his method, refusing to engage mentally and provide him with answers, instead insisting he observe a lot more carefully, and work to concentrate on observing and imitating better. What he would respond with would look like a shallow imitation, to my Kathakali-trained aesthetic sensibility his response felt as a kind of mimicry. I was very troubled and upset by what seemed to me at that time as a conscious trivialisation of the Kathakali form. While he took his own psychophysical work seriously and worked at it very precisely, he seemed to be throwing away very casually the sociopsychophysical image on offer.

Perhaps my defensiveness was also personal, in that I felt his casual gestures were a wider comment on an art form that I had worked at so seriously, and loved, that his was a judgement on the imitative aspects of my culture, implying a hierarchical difference between our two cultures, one of a new migrant and the other of a resident Australian. This had the potential of going the wrong way and ending the relationship. I realised I had to work harder to make it work. For our relationship to survive, I had to do two things: argue more forcefully the value of the mirroring process as well as make my demonstration a very precise step-by-step evocation of the Kathakali form, to repeatedly draw him out of his introverted psychophysicality and into my sociopsychophysical presence, but to work at his pace not mine. Towards this end, I isolated each element of every integrated gestural action and worked with Peter to observe, imitate and repeat it precisely. I then worked harder to integrate it and put it together, working sometimes one-on-one for four hours continuously. Peter was extremely generous through this process, took on this challenge, allowing me to lead and later offered an appreciation of this process.

Peter's response to one-on-one training

So, it was very helpful for me and I felt very grateful that you introduced the one-on-one which helped me work without feeling like throwing in the towel. It's a bit like I've experienced it with computer lessons too, you go to a computer class and the first five minutes you are lost, the rest of the session you feel like weeping, because you are so far back that you will never catch up. So, I appreciated that, and I appreciated your emphasis on letting you judge what was needed. I thought that was wise, and I happened to at the same time be doing one-on-one yoga where the teacher was trying to work out what would suit me and she decided that yielding (laughs) is what would suit me, as my tendency is to work hard, push hard at getting something right which is often the way to get it wrong, so I thought that was invaluable, and that perhaps relates to the idea of mirroring. I read something just the other day about Alexander[3] where he was saying (maybe it was someone else quoting him) something to the effect that one does not always have the embodied knowledge of how to do what you want to do, and so, sometimes you need to find another path to do it. So, I think the idea of letting you be the judge of what was needed, not getting too neurotic or egocentric, or hardworking about getting everything accurate, something like that, I found that very helpful.

(Interview with Peter, June 2016)

Working with Peter gave me a deeper reflection on Kathakali pedagogy. The Kathakali master practitioner leads and leads precisely, offering specific actions to be imitated by the learner. These specific actions need to be imitated with precision and not be interpreted. This precise mirroring of actions leads the learner, over a period of time, through a communion with the master practitioner, into a state of deeper "psychic" engagement. Use of the phrase psychic engagement references an interpretation of *rasa* as existing in the *Natyashastra*. The following passage from the *Natyashastra*, as translated by Pollock, describes the phenomenology of performing a range of emotions, suggesting that there exists a shared essence behind the playing of a range of emotions, what it terms as "psychic sensitivity."

> Psychic sensitivity as defined here is something that arises from the mind; it is said to be the mind in a state of heightened awareness, since the psychic sensitivity arises when the mind is thus aware. The particular nature of each of its different emotions, such as horripilation, weeping, pallor, and the like, cannot be brought about when the actor's mind is elsewhere. Given that the drama imitates the nature of the world, the role of the psychic sensitivity is essential. An example: the dramatic emotions that are effects of pleasure or pain should be purified by psychic sensitivity that they are identical. In the case of pain, for example, which consists of weeping and the like, how can it be acted out by someone not feeling pain; or pleasure, which consists of joy and the like, by someone not feeling pleasure? It is precisely thanks to the actor's psychic sensitivity that he is able, even when not feeling pleasure or

---

3 Frederick Matthias Alexander was an Australian actor who in the first part of the twentieth century developed the Alexander technique, helping actors break through embodied habits by a realignment of the head, neck and body.

pain, to display horripilation or weeping, and it is for this reason that these emotions have been explained as being psychophysical.

(55)

This psychic sensitivity behind the playing of emotional states is the essence of *rasa*. It is that pleasurable taste of an essence or common state of being that lies behind the playing of a range of emotions, each different from the other.

The master practitioner then, through a precise and deep understanding of his embodied practice, passes onto the learner this ability to experience psychic sensitivity. This psychic sensitivity, or more precisely psychophysical sensitivity, exists in the mind, and, I argue, in the body, as a taste of aesthetic pleasure. The Kathakali performer develops a mental psychic sensitivity as well as an embodied psychophysical pleasure. It is for this reason that the Kathakali *guru* needs to lead, his body needs to be imitated precisely because, through mirroring all the choreographed routines and enactments, a specific psychophysical ability is being passed on from master practitioner to learner. This imitative process extends to even a mirroring of the breath of the *guru*, and the breathing patterns of the characters he is enacting.

In the following excerpt from Helen's interview at the end of the 22-month process, she speaks of her experience in India and of observing Pillai teach:

> I noticed I was observing much more detail and I got to the point where I could almost imagine what it is like to be him doing it, I could see how he was breathing and see the angle of the body and where the head was and it was much more of an embodied experience.

She goes on to make the following observation after having watched and trained with videos she recorded of Pillai. Reflecting on how a demonstration by a *guru* can become a shared experience, she adds:

> When we were in India watching students training I couldn't understand still why they were so intently watching him, even as they were doing the dance, because they clearly knew it, and he was demonstrating it from his chair, and I thought they are watching him in case they forgot something, though they did not look like forgetting, they were so on top of the dance, but it is only when I came back and I was practising by myself and I made this observation that I was noticing so much more, his angle and his breathing and I could understand why this movement is like this now, noticing so much more, and then I remembered them watching and I thought "aha" this is what they were observing, they are not just observing the outer form, they are really watching just all the minute details that you can only observe while doing, like he has got an amazing sense of rhythm, even as he is sitting you can almost understand the point at which he turns by observing. All these amazing details, they're good. They are observing all of this. So that for me is mirroring. When you are mirroring far more than the surface.

(Interview, Helen Smith 2016)

Helen's observations suggest that the act of observation is a force on its own in Kathakali learning. It requires an uninterrupted sustained phase of watching the teacher carefully, observing and imitating precise actions, and not mentally interpreting and mimicking the action, for a successful mirroring of dramatic actions to happen. Within the context of actor training, "mentalist" processes on the other hand work through a conscious separation of the mind from the body, setting up the western actor's mind/body split. This method is in contrast to the embodied processes that offer the eastern actor an integrated psychophysicality. In refusing to answer Helen and Peter's questions, in refusing to give them answers to their rational enquiries, in insisting on the demonstration, observation and enactment methodology, I was attending to the need to integrate the western mind body/psycho physical split, wherein a mental engagement precedes a physical enactment. By demanding a sustained observation of my demonstrations, conditions for an embodied communion and an integrated psychophysicality were being created. This integration empowers the actor to act meaningfully, intentionally, dramatically and with embodied pleasure.

As Helen describes so vividly, when a Kathakali learner is observing a *guru* teach, she is empathetically watching actions not only for their physical and motor reality, but even further for their intentions and objectives or "end goals." This "deep brained" process of "action observation," "action intention" and "end goal" realisation is a process of embodied integration between the observer and the observed. This unselfconscious sustained observation of the teacher (and other master performers), especially in a one-on-one situation, is the essence of the sociopsychophysical offering of Kathakali. It comes from the sustained social relationship between learner and teacher. In Kathakali actor training, the social informs both the pedagogy, as well as the text and performativity. The social binds the performer's psychophysical into an integrated whole.

It is for this wholeness, at the first instance, that Zarrilli and the psychophysical tradition engage with Asian forms, working to solve the Cartesian duality of a mind/body split. Responding to Wallace in an interview, Zarrilli here clarifies:

> At a philosophical level, I think Asian thought is very, very useful because there is no bodymind duality in certain Asian philosophical traditions. In the West we do have the unfortunate legacy of Cartesian dualism and that is something that is so ingrained in Anglo-American culture in the way that we think, act, are inculturated, that makes it very difficult to get over. Having encountered things in non-Western cultures provides models and conceptual frameworks for a way to problem-solve and to do it clearly for people, not by romanticising, but by challenging certain ways of thinking in the West that are problematic for actors. If somebody wants to be a dualist, [fine], but if you want to be an actor it is not going to help you. It is a pragmatic issue.
>
> (Zarrilli Interview 24 February) (Wallace 2012:112)

Within the Kathakali world, this integration of the learner's mind and body is realised through the *guru shishya* pedagogy, and the very intimate social nature of this relationship. In the traditional world of the old social, caste belonging framed *guru shishya* relationships. In the martial art *kalaripayattu* training, for example, you would have a *nair guru* training a *nair shishya*. This commonality feeds a social intimacy, a oneness, a social non-separateness. This oneness facilitates an embodied intersubjective communion.

In his TED talk (2009), it is to the intersubjective embodied communion that neuroscientist Ramachandran brings attention when mooting human connectivity, playfully referring to what he terms as "Gandhi Neurons" or "empathy neurons," while articulating the neuroscience of human intersubjective communion. In the human brain, mirror neurons facilitate this embodied communion. An understanding of mirror neurons and the mirror neuron system helps further nuance an understanding of the "deep brained" processes of actor training and psychic sensitivity articulated in the *Natyashastra*. In the next section, I work to understand the mirror neuron system and its relevance with respect to Kathakali mirroring.

Kathakali mirroring and the mirror neuron system

Mirror neurons are not "magic cells." Their significance lies in their ability to integrate while operating on information received from other brain areas: aural, visual, affective, motor. This integration or communion happens within the motor system, that system in the brain that brings us, through our motor acts, out of ourselves as it were and into the world of others. In the present context, these motor acts are the actions of a Kathakali drama. These externalising and socialising properties inherent within the mirror neuron system create a potential for the body to perform motor actions. By actions are implied not just general body movements or even specific motor acts but, in effect, the integration of motor acts with their social intentionality or an "end goal" as directed towards their outer social world. This integrated process may then be termed "action intentionality." An ability to read and respond to "action intentionality" is inherent in the MNS as demonstrated when mirror neurons fired even as the action observed was only partially visible (Umlita et al. 2001), or when an associated sound or visual image was observed (Kohler et al. 2002).

In Kathakali mirroring, the learner observes the motor actions of the teacher but in so doing also absorbs the dramatic intention and intensity of that action. While observing an action, the brain is also recognising the intention of that action, and seeing it for its entirety, seeing the action even as it is being enacted to its logical conclusion. "Action observation" as facilitated by the MNS is not merely a visual recorder and facilitator of an imitation of another's motor act, but also a predictor of the inherent intentionality of the motor act. It is as if a single motor neuron not only observes acts but also acts intentionally executing the end goal of the motor act, operating as an integrated neural process that reveals a meaningful outward social engagement via the social gestural intentionality of the motor act. In this manner, the mirror neuron system facilitates both the coding of an observed action's intentionality as well as its outer motor expression.

Kathakali learning works by the learner observing the teacher's motor acts. However, as described above and earlier documented by Helen observing subtle details of breathing patterns, the learner observes not just the motor act, but even its intentionality and its end goal. The Kathakali *guru* teaches both the motor actions, and the emotions and intentions and objectives of the character he is demonstrating. The learner at each moment of learning is observing a complete and meaningful dramatic action. When the learner imitates precisely a motor action, an integrated set of dramatic values, actions, emotions and intentions, including an ease and pleasure of performing those actions or *rasa*, is being learnt.

To conclude, when the Kathakali *guru* demonstrates an action, he initiates an entire cycle of observation, imitation and repetition. Each element of this cycle has its own logic and needs to be performed to its fullest. The demonstration needs to be dramatic with the motor action integrated with the intention, emotion and end goal of the action. The observation must be concentrated and sustained, the imitation precise, and the repetition rigorous enough for the action to be absorbed into the performer's deep brain space. With Helen and Peter, through the course of our conflicts and struggles, it was possible to follow this traditional Kathakali pedagogy. The end goal of this cycle of integration is then the performer's experience of aesthetic pleasure or *rasa*.

In the next chapter I work though the social aspect of the sociopsychophysical, locating Kathakali texts and performativity within the seventeenth-century social world and its culture of caste and untouchability. Through a reading of available literature on anthropology, history, culture and caste, I identify the role of the *nair* warrior caste that first performed Kathakali, and, from their martial identity, frame a theme of Kathakali's "gestures of embodied aggression." These gestures when performed to complex rhythms or *taalam*s in an intercultural exercise, as discussed in Chapter 7, bring pleasure or *rasa* to the western performer.

6 Caste, Kathakali and its "gestures of embodied aggression"

In this chapter, four seventeenth-century Kathakali texts and their performativity are contextualised within their social world and the principles and culture that drive it. Theoretical frameworks are set up using debates in the social sciences around the values and structure of the caste system. While focussing on the role and function of the *nair* caste that first performed Kathakali in the seventeenth century, four Kathakali classics written by Kottayam Thamburan, the ruler of the princely state of Kottayam in Kerala, are referred to, with greater attention to one of them, *Kalayana Saugandhikam* or "The Flower of Good Fortune." An understanding and interpretation of these texts was received by me from six Kathakali teachers and noted down by me in my learning diaries. Kottayyam Thampuran (c. 1645–1716) wrote and created the first four classics of Kathakali using his *kalaripayattu*-trained *nair* soldiers.

The real caste equation, between the ruler Kottayam Thampuran, the warrior *nair* community and the dominating *nambudiri brahmin* caste, helps frame an understanding of the inter-caste relations setting up an appreciation of the performing power of the *nair* performer and his performative gestures of embodied aggression. These gestures of embodied aggression emerge from the values of domination and aggression embedded into the warrior *nair* caste that Kathakali was traditionally performed by. These gestures of embodied aggression are directed not only at other characters on stage but further onto the social space of the audience. These gestures come from the role of the *nair* caste whose place and purpose in the caste hierarchy, in the seventeenth century, was to dominate and control the hierarchical social order (Figure 6.1).

By this elaboration of the social weave, implicated into this chapter are three important binding principles and values that frame the debates in the social sciences around the Indian caste system: values of purity and impurity (Dumont 1970); empirical and conceptual interrelationships (Veena Das 1977); and socio-economic dominance (Guha 2013).

Purity, and impurity are, for Dumont, the defining values of occupations that work their way up and down the social hierarchy; the higher up you go, the more pure a function you perform – for example, you conduct the prayer service in the temple. While, on the other hand, the lower you go, the more impure the function, for example, the skinning of the carcasses of dead animals to create leather.

Figure 6.1 A gesture of embodied aggression: Raudra (raging) Bhima (Kottakkal Kesevan Kundlayar) challenging Dussassana to a fight.

For Das, the simplicity and clarity of Dumont's binary structure is complicated by each caste; for instance, a *brahmin* priest or *kshatriya* king are both empirical entities as well as structural categories of Hindu thought. For Das, simple binary equations of purity and impurity, when used to define inter-caste equations, prove inadequate. For her, the tripartite division between the "priest," the "king" and the "householder" and its other, the "ascetic," for example, serves as a more stable tool of enquiring into caste roles and realities. In certain existential circumstances, the purer *brahmin* priest may be lower in status than the less pure *kshatriya* king, while in others, the *brahmin* may be higher. Thus, caste equations are interchangeable for Das and emerge through the particular circumstances and existential conditions that these interrelationships occupy. No single holistic plan, as is Dumont's, frames the caste order. It is imperative then for a negotiation of caste to be both empirical as well as conceptual. As empirical conditions are very complex in the field, as this chapter will elaborate, my primary working methodology is conceptual.

For Guha, whose recent work (2013) has been appreciated by social scientists for its offer of a new paradigm, the structure of the caste system depends less on the religious cultural values of purity and impurity and more on the socioeconomic necessity of protecting clusters of villages and their economic and social activity, and this dictates the particular nature and function of a caste. A caste group shares the culture and value of dominance or protection, as the case may be. This theoretical construct works well in the context of the seventeenth-century *nair* caste whose main function was to defend land and territory, and by implication, the king or *thampuran*.

A theoretical understanding of caste and a negotiation around these debates enriches our appreciation of seventeenth-century Kathakali texts and performativity framing an understanding of the *nair* caste's dominating role in the social weave, a role that generates its gestures of embodied aggression. These gestures of embodied aggression have as their socially embodied other, gestures of embodied submission. These gestures of embodied aggression, emerging from a caste contextualisation of Kathakali text and performativity, are a valuable tool in working with performers in Australia as evidenced in the next chapter, drawing as they do the psychophysically introverted performer into the social space of performance.

In the context of Kathakali actor training, an understanding of these gestures of embodied aggression/submission may begin right from the ritual of feet touching that initiates each learning session. The learner submits to the embodied presence of the teacher by bending low and touching his/her feet. While in most circles of a shared culture, as between a similar caste, family or community, this ritual is conducted obediently, its abstract meaning and inherent embodied aggression/submission are revealed in conflict and resistance. The moment of touch may then be seen as potentially the bridging moment between a gesture of embodied aggression, the teacher's embodied presence demanding respect, and an expected acquiescence by the learner facilitating an inclusion. That the *guru* allows the learner to touch his body, and that too the lowest part, is significant. Gabriele (2008) connects the act of touch within the wider culture of untouchability:

> The abolition of "untouchability" as a political and social practice has not yet changed completely the individual perception of touch, which is strongly linked to the concept of pollution. Avoidance of contact and touch with persons or objects classified as impure is a prominent feature of Indian society and is intrinsically linked with core values, such as status, purity and power. Public demonstrations of "intimate" touch, such as kissing, are unacceptable and, if displayed, lead to a storm of indignation, as the emotions excited by the Richard Gere/Shilpa Shetty (*an actress Gere kissed publicly*) case illustrates. Given the importance attributed to rules of the avoidance of touch, the

question arises, what about touch? When is touch practised? What is considered touch and what constitutes it? And what does it mean, as both a personal experience and a public symbol? Is touch just the absence of "untouchability"? And if so, does it then signify status equality? Or is touch coded and structured like the rules of "untouchability"?

(524–525, my italics)

Aware of the complexity of touch as described in the quote above this thesis seeks to provoke a renegotiation of this traditional practice of feet touching in the context of teaching Kathakali to contemporary performers in Australia.

While touching of the *guru*'s feet may be seen as an embodied gesture of respect, contextualised within the Indian caste system, this practice is complicated. As Veena Das observes:

In the famous Purusa Sukta, which describes the origin of the four varnas, the body is divided horizontally and hierarchically, with the Brahmans emerging from the head, the Kshatriyas from the arms, the Vaishyas from the thighs and the Shudras from the feet of the primeval man. This hierarchical division of the body serves as a suitable metaphor for the hierarchical division of society into four *varnas*.

(1977:126)

Within this specific conceptual construct, when a learner bends to touch the teacher's feet, she is paying obeisance to this social order, accepting her place alongside what is conceptually the space of the *shudra*, within a shared culture of untouchability. The teacher is now the head of the embodied encryption or conceptually a *brahmin*. If the teacher were to disallow his feet being touched through a message of no touch, the learner would be excluded from the learning space. The excluded learner would then exist outside the social space as an outcaste/conceptually an untouchable. A model of such a social space could be framed in phenomenological terms as touch–no touch–untouchable.

This construct of touch–no touch–untouchable may be used to examine the social inclusion or exclusion of characters in Kathakali dance dramas. In her essay entitled "The Good, the Bad and the Ugly: Kathakali's Females and the Men Who Play Them," Marlene B. Pitkow structures the female character in Kathakali according to varying degrees of inclusion within the social order. The "Good" is the honourable married woman at the centre of the social order. The "Bad" is the outcaste woman who is still allowed in, or finds her way into the social circle. The "Ugly" is the outcaste and untouchable woman, who may only appear as an uncontrolled monstress/demoness (2011:223–243). The good woman then is the very touchable woman. The bad is the one not to be touched but allowed into the social space. The ugly is the untouchable one to be violated for any attempts at entering the social space.

This construct of touch–no touch–untouchable may also be used to structure characters from the plays by Kottayam Thamburan. In the seventeenth-century

Kathakali drama *Kirmira Vadham*, available in English through a translation by Zarrilli (2000a:118–130), the story adapted from the *Mahabharata* has the *pandavas* exiled into the forest with a thousand *brahmins* following them as an entourage. These *brahmins* need to be fed by Draupadi, a problem she resolves by praying to the god Krishna. In a subplot, Draupadi is enticed to travel deeper into the forest by a demoness *simhika* dressed up as a beautiful woman *lalitha*. Her plan is to abduct Draupadi and eat her up. In this story, the "Good" is the touchable *minnuku* character type like Draupadi, the Pandava wife. Her central dilemma is to feed a thousand hungry *brahmins*, a very touchable task, as the pure *brahmins* are happy to eat food touched by her hands. The "Bad," *lalita* character is the (no touch) not to be touched female demon *simhika* in disguise as a beautiful maiden. Draupadi makes the almost fatal error of befriending her, touching her. She is abducted by the demoness who wants to kill/eat her. The demoness now reveals her true form as the untouchable, "Ugly," *kari* character type, a grotesque and vile creature who is punished by Draupadi's husband Bhīma, for transgressing, for touching and abducting Draupadi. Her nose and breasts are cut off. She leaves the stage screaming in pain.

In another of the four golden classics titled "The Flower of Good Fortune," while seeking permission from his brother Yudhishthira to fight the enemy, a raging Bhīma begins by first touching his brother's feet, recognising and paying obeisance to his place in the hierarchical order. Through the scene, even as Bhīma rages, seeking revenge and threatening his enemy with gestures of embodied aggression, Yudhishthira, a *kshatriya* like Bhīma, plays the role of calm wise *brahmin*. In the next scene, when a violated and molested Draupadi, with her hair left untouched, untied and open, asks her husband to go bring her *saugandhika* flowers, she is in the no touch space, she does not touch him nor let herself be touched, the husband and wife do not hold hands or display any affection. Only when Bhīma is leaving for the forest do they formally embrace, barely touching each other, with the elaborate costume and makeup facilitating the delicacy of the liminal touch–no touch space. Later in the play when Hanuman, the monkey god, lies down and blocks Bhīma's path, Bhīma, by refusing to touch him, to hold his tail and remove him from the path, by expressing contempt for his lowly status, treats him in a way that conceptually may be understood as treating an untouchable.

By these examples of touch–no touch–untouchable I initiate an inquiry into discovering caste-related codes of behaviour within Kathakali text and performativity.

Background

Key scholarship in English on Kathakali does not engage with the complexity of caste, either in the form itself or in the lived experience of it. Iyer (1955); Pandaya (1961); Jones and True (1970); Zarrilli (1984, 1992, 2000a, 2000b, 2004, 2009, 2013); Schechner (1988); Barba (1995) and Pitkow (1998) neglect the complexity of caste in Kathakali, i.e., the lived experience of it. While Zarrilli in fair detail describes the role of the *nair* or *kshatriya* caste as well as more generally the social order, and while Pitkow attends to the feminine representation, including lower-caste female and demonic characters, the lived experience and interrelation of one caste vis-à-vis another are little remarked upon, probably because this study of inter-caste relationship may be perceived as contentious, and is difficult to negotiate for someone who has not experienced caste as part of their lived experience.

In his article titled "Contested Narratives on and off the *Kathakali* Dance-Drama Stage," Zarrilli recognises, in the context of Kerala's leftist government policy makers and their attempts at critiquing and transforming the traditional temple-based arts with the aim of facilitating an ideologically sound contemporary reinvention, "the potential enmity of those whose personal caste-specific identity is invested in the powerful, highly public symbols of caste-specific performance traditions like *teyyam* or *kathakali*" (1992:111). Zarrilli is correct in his observation. In Kerala, each individual ritual, folk, classical art form belonged to a particular group, community or caste whose identity was and continues to be deeply connected to it. Any critique of the art form or reinvention needs to traverse the difficult edge of negotiating that sense of deep-rooted caste or community-based ownership. The difficulty is heightened when that community is the researcher's host.

Additionally, caste-related fieldwork in India for an Indian researcher is a problematic business too, due to conflicting caste identities. I, for example, am an upper-caste Kashmiri *brahmin*, and any overt display of this fact may have consequences. Travelling in a metro in Gurgaon, India, recently (January, 2016), I realised a complete obliteration of caste identity. No one cared or knew who sat down next to whom. Overtly asking after someone's caste identity, in principle, is not acceptable in today's urban India. Yet, its politics and social life, especially in rural India, are driven in large measure by caste, making it a significant context for the understanding of a practice like Kathakali.

Sumit Guha, in his recent work *Beyond Caste Identity and Power in South Asia, Past and Present* (2013), argues convincingly that an understanding of caste is best served by engaging with ideas of power and domination. For Guha, a status-ranked ethnic community or caste became in South Asia "a highly involuted, politicized form of ethnic ranking shaped by the constant exercise of socio-economic power" (Guha 2013:2). A caste then is defined by its place in the order of dominance and the culture and values shared within the group.

For French social anthropologist Louis Dumont, in his seminal if much critiqued work entitled *Homo Hierarchus* (1970), caste is best understood through a religio-cultural model based on a single true principle, namely the opposition of the pure and impure. In *Homo Hierarchus*, Dumont works to integrate into a single idea three founding principles of the caste order: (1) hierarchy, (2) separation and (3) a division of labour.

> These three "principles," rest on one fundamental conception and are reducible to a single true principle, namely the opposition of the pure and impure.

> This opposition underlies hierarchy, which is the superiority of the pure to the impure, underlies separation because the pure and the impure must be kept separate, and underlies the division of labor because pure and impure occupations must likewise be kept separate. The whole is founded on the necessary and hierarchical co-existence of the two opposites.
>
> (1970:43)

Both Guha's socioeconomic power domination on the one hand and Dumont's hierarchically[1] ordered religio-cultural values of pure/impure on the other serve well as frames of reference in my present endeavour.

The difficulty of any holistic attempt at a caste contextualisation of Kathakali text and performativity, however, lies in the absence of two out of the four castes from the four dramas mentioned. The stories of gods and demons and kings and queens include *brahmins* or priests and *kshatriyas* or warriors, but they neglect the *vaisyas* or merchants and the *shudras* or labourers/untouchables. Yet, these unrepresented castes were there at the periphery of the audience space; the inclusivity of Kathakali, towards all castes, is argued for by Sadanam Balakrishan (2005:95).[2] By working conceptually rather than empirically, I negotiate the *vaisyas* and *shudras* absence/presence once again in phenomenological terms. The onstage presence of the *nairs* I call "being there." The audiences I place as "being there/not being there" (actually present centrally and peripherally, but fictively and performatively absent as with *vaisyas*). The "highly polluting" untouchable castes I frame as "not there." The complications of the under-researched caste composition of the traditional seventeenth-century audience may then be framed in phenomenological terms as "there-being there, not being there-not there." This convoluted phenomenological construct acknowledges the ambiguity and complexity of the onstage/audience composition, though there is a sense, acknowledged by Zarrilli, that for a Kathakali performance "more if not all were present" (2000a:6).

Working through Macquarrie and Edward's (1973) translation of *Being and Time*, Heidegger's concept of "Being" is particularly useful here. As a performer and a Kashmiri *brahmin* writing of my lived experience of both Kathakali

1 In the context of the performing arts in Kerala, the top of Dumont's hierarchy has *kutiyattam* performed by a caste of *brahmin* temple servants or *chakyars*, the lowest rung of "untouchables" have their form of deity possession *theyyam*, and the interstitial space is occupied by the *nair* community performing Kathakali.

2 "During the nineteenth and early twentieth centuries, landlords considered it a matter of pride to organize and conduct performances in their courtyards. For a Kathakali performance during such occasions, invitations were not necessary. Keli, the percussion announcement on the evening of the performance, would draw the community to the site of the drama to be enacted later that night. There was, and still is, no restriction or bar on who could attend a Kathakali play. The inclusiveness is one of the principal strengths of this art form, and it has contributed to its survival and popularity. Kathakali is a theatre for everyone – for the young and old, for lower and higher castes, and for communities of all persuasions" (Balakrishnan 2005:95).

practice and the Indian caste system, an exploration into the essence or being of the Kathakali performer is needed for, as Heidegger's philosophy has alerted us, "We are ourselves the entities to be analyzed. The Being of any such entity is in each case mine" (Macquarrie and Robinson (trans) 1973:67). I seek the meaning of my own embodied practice within the performativity of Kathakali on the stage. I interpret Heidegger's Being as the individual essence of the Kathakali practitioner (myself).

The value of engaging my caste-embodied being with this scholarly exercise may best be understood by an example of a personal experience, my own reaction/anger towards one of my Kathakali teachers when he physically hit me. My rage at being hit with the rhythm stick at the age of 30, on reflection 22 years later as I write this, was a *brahmin*'s rage. Even after being hit, I continued dancing. I stamped my feet violently, danced and gestured angrily in what I can only define as a crazed Rumpelstiltskin-like fashion. On reflection, now years later, I recognise my gestural display as similar to the performative expression of a *brahmin*'s curse. In Kathakali's source literature, the epic *Mahabharata*, while *kshatriyas* rage to kill, *brahmins* curse. While the biophysical texture of rage is unequivocally similar across human bodies/castes, its performed expression across culture differs. *Brahmin* characters on stage rage differently to *kshatriyas* because the end product of rage is different. *Brahmins* curse, *kshatriyas* kill. Even formally, text-based *kutiyattam* is performed by upper-caste temple servants, with the actor reciting/chanting text, and represents conceptually a theatrical space of the *brahmin*'s curse. A curse is a set of words/text spoken harshly. Kathakali's embodied dance, physicality and aggression, further enhanced by a silent non-speaking warrior performer, reflect the *kshatriya* function to kill. This sequence further begs the question of the absent *dalit* or untouchable's rage. Though outside the scope of the present enquiry, it is relevant to note here that states of deity possession in *theyyam* reflect the repressed emotional anger/pain of the untouchable. By these insights, I suggest the value of using my caste-encrypted social being and identity as a tool of enquiry and knowledge gathering.

To make specific the embodied culture of caste, Heidegger's ideas on touch are particularly useful and relevant. He observes: "When entities are 'worldless' in themselves, they can never 'touch' each other, nor can either of them be alongside each other" (Macquarrie and Robinson (trans) 1973:81). Touching establishes the existence of a shared destiny, being in a common world. To be alongside each other, Heidegger frames the individual's existence as "being-in-the-world" with the "being-in" having "the-world" alongside it. The two entities then may touch each other as they are alongside each other and are "encounterable" (Macquarrie and Robinson (trans) 1973:81). This encounter happens in a shared world. The act of touching establishes the existence of a shared destiny, with the entities touching and touched encountering themselves within that world and by that act of touch. Within this framework, in such a shared world, the culture of untouchability includes an interrelationship defined by a culture of touch–no touch–untouchable.

This interrelationship is between the one, with the power to touch, and the other, with no power to touch. The culture of untouchability then is, by the act of dictating the rights over the encounter, the establishing of an ownership of a shared world.

At this stage of the enfolding argument I revisit ideas presented in the previous chapter that would explain the difficulty of negotiating issues and practices of untouchability. I refer again to Leder's ideas of "absence" and Bourdieu's "habitus," theorized in the previous chapters. As the caste-encrypted body exists as an absence, with the head conceptually deemed as *brahmin,* and the foot *shudra,* the abstracted meanings of cultural practices like those of feet touching, that emerge from this encryption, remain absent from consciousness. As practices leading you to an inclusion into the power structures of the social space, as "habitus," they work unconsciously, complicating an investigation into their social meaning.

As discussed earlier, the culture of untouchability includes an interrelationship of touch–no touch–untouchable. In the upper–lower caste–untouchable power/ domination equation, this interrelationship is between the one with the power to touch, and the other, with no power to touch. The former, as the teacher does in the learning space, establishes an ownership of the shared world. Also helpful here is Veena Das' insightful analysis of Sanskrit texts, which contributes to a deeper understanding of caste-related interrelationships in the context of Kathakali texts and performativity. In it, she includes the tripartite interrelationship of the priest (*brahmin*)–king (*kshatriya*) and the social householder/asocial ascetic (*sanayasi*) (Das 1977:7). The demons in Kathakali dramas may be seen as the forest other of the ascetic or *sanyasi.* Conceptually, as structures of Hindu thought, these categories represent all significant characters and relationships in the four classics of Kathakali.

Finally, it should be noted that a localised form of the caste system known as *jati* exists in Kerala (Sadasivan 2000; Ghurye 1969). It is to a local variant of the *jati* system that the King of Kottayam, Kottayyam Thamburan, the writer and choreographer of the first four classics of Kathakali, belonged. As a monarch, was Kottayam Thamburan higher in status than all other *jatis*? In her extensive coverage of the caste composition of Kerala society, Kathleen Gough details the caste status and compositions of the higher *jatis,* the *nambudiris* and the *nair* (also spelt *nayars*). The former were equivalent to the *brahmins* of the *varna* system, ranked "ritually above the Kings and were to some extent above and outside the political systems of the Kingdoms" (Gough and Schneider 1961:306). Dumont notes hegemonic *brahmin* empowerment in south India as well: "Thus in the south there are scarcely any castes intermediate between Brahman and Shudras; the warrior castes themselves are considered as part of the Shudras" (1970:73). *Shudra,* as the feet of the caste body, represents the labouring body as always lower in power and status.

By this conception in South India, even royalty, below the *nambudiri* in power and status, was deemed *shudra.* The *nairs* too, as the *kshatriya* component in this lower class, have further hierarchical divisions of sub-groups. Gough records five discrete *jatis* within the higher *nairs* (spelt by her as *nayars*) each with their discrete purpose. These included in decreasing order of status and power "Kiriattil Nayars, Vellayma Nayars, Purattu Nayar, Agattu Nayars, Pallichan Nayars and Sudra Nayars" (Gough and Schneider 1961:308–309). Below these, as Gough and Schneider document, were the *nair* temple servants with "degrading" occupations: "*Chidigans* – funeral priests, *Veluttedans* – washermen of the castes above them and *Vilakkataravans* – barbers of all the castes above them" (311). Therefore, even if Kathakali was performed and seen by only one community of *nairs*, the reality of lower groups both within and without the *nairs* was present in the Kathakali audience. The conceptual idea and existential identity of being lower in caste ran all the way through the caste hierarchy, starting from the lowest untouchable and moving right up to the highest *nambudiri brahmin*, i.e., except for the highest *brahmin* everyone one else was lower in caste to someone else.

Within this hierarchised social structure, caste identity and social belonging restricted social mobility. Roles assigned to each individual being within the caste system worked not only to define their social existence but also to effectively restrict the existential potential for their self-realisation – not in a spiritual sense of the ascetic but in terms of social role. The carpenter's son had no option but to be a carpenter and the night soil carrier's child would be a night soil carrier. In the seventeenth century, such social conditions (see Gough and Schneider 1961:298–415) were unequivocally the site of Kathakali performativity.

In such a caste-inscribed social world, Kottayyam Thampuran used his soldiers and controllers of the area belonging to the *nair* caste to be the first Kathakali dancers, and the movement vocabulary of the dance was based on martial training. Lower sub castes were present even in the limited audience of only one community. In a Kathakali performance in the seventeenth century, when a lower caste first saw an actor on stage he would have recognised both the Kathakali performer as the character he was presenting but also as the *nair* warrior he was by caste. These warriors were trained in gymnasiums or *kalaris* through the martial art form *kalaripayattu*. As Zarrilli observes:

> Kathakali's vigorous choreography, its tremendously powerful and masculine leaps and jumps, and perhaps even its stylized battle choreography were all drawn from the actor's physical abilities developed in the rigorous martial training programme, as well as directly from movement patterns and models taken from the martial system.
>
> (1984:54)

The form and structure of the embodied dance on the Kathakali stage is a ritualisation of an attack or retreat response. When I studied with him in the 1990s, Sadanam Balakrishnan would insist on this rigorous back-and-forth movement of the choreography, which often gets diluted in performance due to the heavy weight of the costume. On stage, performers take two steps back, and two forward, instead of four steps each way. This reduction dilutes the attack and retreat martial element of the form.

As Evoor Rajendran Pillai, Principal of the International Centre for Kathakali in New Delhi observed in an interview:

> The Kathakali dancer is never still. He is always moving. This movement is essentially either downstage, towards the audience or it is returning upstage. All the aggressive gestures are directed downstage while all the gentler gestures are performed upstage.
>
> (Pillai 2016)

His principal dancers, Kalanilayam Jagadeeshan Thiruvatta and Kalamadalam Anil Kumar, concurred that the back-and-forth movement may be perceived as *yuddham-shantam* (war and peace), and this was the overarching theme under which all Kathakali scenes/choreography might also be placed. Kathakali gestures are spatially located and performed along a vertical upstage/downstage axis. Gestures/*mudras* that are about relief, rest and wellbeing (i.e., house, king, gods, flowers, joy) are all performed with a leap back, moving upstage away from the audience. Gestures that evoke aggression (i.e., enemy, destroy, cruel) are performed moving forward with an embodied aggression directed downstage towards the audience (Zarrilli 1984:131–132; Balakrishnan 2005:138).

This choreography helps the performer embody the constant tension and release, or what I term attack and retreat, serving the alternating thematic impulses of war and peace. These playful ritualised actions of the Kathakali performer are gestures of embodied aggression directed towards both other characters on stage as well as the audience. It is to be remembered that each gesture of embodied aggression was played out to a specific rhythm or *taalam*, setting up within this project a challenging level of skill and ability for the western performer.

A case study: "The Flower of Good Fortune"

To offer a specific example of these social gestures of embodied aggression, I analyse choreography from "The Flower of Good Fortune." The choreography of this particular set piece, almost unchanged, and from the seventeenth-century classic *Kalyana Saugandhikam* is traditionally used for actor training, and is the most challenging piece for a student actor and the culmination of his training. In Scene 1, Bhīma the great warrior is asking permission from his brother, King Yudhishthira, to take revenge on his enemy Dussassana, whose chest he has sworn to tear open, and whose blood he has sworn to drink. Here, Bhīma is in the attack mode (standing) while Yudhishthira is in the retreat mode (sitting). Emotionally too Bhīma is in a rage while Yudhishthira is calm. Bhīma is the *Kshatriya* warrior, while Yudhishthira is taking on the virtues of a wise man, conceptually a *brahmin*. At the start of this scene, a *shloka* or narrative song introduces the episode and then, as the hand-held curtain is lowered, it reveals Bhīma doing a short aggressive pose, while twice standing menacingly on one leg, first at the upstage end away from the audience and, second, at the downstage end near the audience. Having established these points of reference, the dialogue begins and the back-and-forth attack or retreat action continues till the end, when Bhīma sits at the downstage point and demonstrates how he will, with his bare hands, tear open his enemy Dussassana's chest and drink his blood.

Significantly, in this version of the story Bhīma does not actually kill his caste cousin Dussassana, he only threatens to do so with a gestural display of aggression.[3] The actual killing is performed in another popular Kathakali drama *Duryodhana Vadham* ("Death of Duryodhana") by Vayaskara Aryan Narayanan Moosad (1841–1902), where Duryodhana is killed by Bhīma on the great bat-tlefield of Kurukshetra. As Jeffery (1976) observes, the mid-nineteenth century was a time that coincided with the fading of both the *nair* caste and Kathakali. During this period, the colonial state and its policies beleaguered and depleted the power of the landed and dominant *nair* caste through a series of land reforms that dwindled their traditional hold over land, encouraging and empowering the lower castes through missionary-led education. A growing capitalist economy where money and industry prevailed over older forms of feudal linkages and hegemony further alienated the *nair* hold over the populace. Perhaps in that era a more literal display of *nair* dominance (i.e., actual killing) was felt necessary, even if the evil doer at the receiving end of *nair* justice was also a *kshatriya/nair*.

Setting up the *nair* warrior's dominant role in the social weave, Kottayam Thampuran's four plays, written in the seventeenth century, avoided the actual battles of the Great War or *Mahabharata*, and suggest the king's intention to cele-brate the *nair* warrior's craft while avoiding showing the killing of caste brothers. For the *nair* community, that period of dominance was a secure one, with lesser confusions and contradictions. Through the logic of his choices and through the celebration of the *nair* caste, the royal can be perceived as subverting a traditional hierarchy that had the *nambudiri* or *brahmin* lording over both the *nair* and the king. However, despite his not showing the actual killing, even Bhīma's gestural demonstration is a ferocious display of his righteous strength as a provider of jus-tice, showing how he will tear open Dussassana's chest with his bare hands and take cannibalistic delight in drinking his blood. This ferocious act of touchability threatens to punish Dussassana for molesting Bhīma's wife Draupadi.

It is not hard then to imagine how Kathakali's aggressive enactments work to dominate the individual viewer, especially those whose caste is below the *nair* warrior/performer. By this, Kathakali's gestures of embodied aggression validate Guha's hypothesis suggesting social domination as the core shared value bind-ing a caste group together. For the *brahmin* caste, for example, these gestures of domination take on the form of a *brahmin*'s curse that damns the all-important *atma* or soul, while for the warrior *kshatriya* or *nair* caste, they translate into

---

3 This is an important distinction between a gestural display of aggression and an actual killing which is reserved for demonic characters. In all the four plays, the *nair/kshatriya* warriors kill no one from within the caste system – no *brahmin* and no lower caste. The only ones to be killed are the caste other – the demons. The rest are to be subdued, threatened, protected or punished through gestures of embodied aggression

gestures of physical threat and violence. Kathakali then embodies and celebrates these social gestures of embodied dominance by the *nair* community and creates out of them a flamboyant dance theatre. This particular role in the social weave gives to the Kathakali performer his open, bold and celebratory gestures that are of value in training actors grown in a more inward, introverted and experimental aesthetic, a point taken up further in Chapter 7. To appreciate this particular texture, it is necessary to delve a little deeper both into its *nair* caste character as well as into its alternative vision of dominance, alternate to the *nambudiri* or *brahmin*. This alternate vision is explored through an interpretation of the four classics of Kathakali and the textual choices made by their inventor Kottayam Thampuran.

Namboodiri dominance of the social weave

In the seventeenth century, *nairs* existed within the hegemonic control of the *nambudiri* landlords who held power over the social order including the religio-temple structures where performances were held. "The greater landlords were managers of large temples, promulgators of religious law, legal advisers of Kings, priests of public sacrifices, or philosophers and Vedic scholars" (Gough and Schneider 1961:306). All the genres that fed into Kathakali were controlled by the temple system. This includes *kutiyattam* performed in temples by *chak-yars* or higher-caste temple servants, *krishnaattam*, a religious art about the god Krishna performed only in the Guruvayur Temple, *theyyam*, a form of deity possession, performed in the temples of, and by the lower untouchable castes, and the immediate precursor to Kathakali, *ramanattam*, telling the stories of the Hindu god Rama (Zarrilli 1984:39–45). Kathakali stepped away from the temple system by being performed in courtyards of rich landlords and village squares (Balakrishnan 2005:95; Zarrilli 2000a:6). Its stories were taken primarily from the *Mahabharata*, which is a more temporal, literary and less god-centric story of a battle between two sets of *kshatriya* cousins. Kottayam Thampuran's four stories, inspired by the *Mahabharata*, have the Pandava brothers as their heroes and the gods playing only a minor role. This elevation of the human helped move the discrete caste identity of the *nairs* away from the religio-temple structures and *brahmin* hegemony.[4]

The first four Kathakali stories present the *nair* warrior in all his power and glory and resist the religio-*brahmin* overlordship which was imprinted on *nair* identity through hypergamous relationships and liaisons. While the eldest son of a *nambudiri* patrilineal extended family had to marry within his caste, preserving

---

4 Quoting a Nayar leader Mannutha Padmanabhan, social historian S.N. Sadasivan observes "Even the all powerful-supreme lord, the sovereign is made to agree that he is untouchable to the Brahmin ... and had to keep a distance of two to three feet from the latter. The prime responsibility of a monarch installed by the Brahmin is the maintenance of the caste system and untouchability" (2000:380).

land and lineage, the younger *nambudiri* sons were allowed liaisons with *nair* women.

> These hypergamous unions were regarded by Brahmins as socially accept-able concubinage, for the union was not initiated with Vedic rites, the chil-dren were not recognised as Brahmins, and neither the woman nor the child was accorded the right of kin.
>
> (Gough and Schneider 1961:320)

However, for the matrilineal *nairs*, these relationships were regarded as mar-riage: "They fulfilled the conditions of ordinary Nayar marriage and served to legitimise the children as an acceptable member of his matrilineal lineage and caste" (320).

Kottayam Thampuran's choice of stories from the *Mahabharata* reflects a cer-tain shifting ground of this *nair nambudiri* relationship. Kottayam Thampuran as a king was not considered a *nair* and, thus, existed in a liminal place, in between the *nambudiri* and the *nair*. His four stories here are interpreted from notes made during my decades-long engagement while learning from Kathakali masters like Sadanam Balakrishnan, Kudamanoor Kalamandalam Nair, Kalamandalam Krishna Kumar and Evoor Rajendran Pillai. These teachers were all *nairs*, includ-ing both higher and lower sub caste *nairs*.

As a Kashmiri *brahmin*, I was equivalent in status in the *varna* system to the *nambudiris* but, as a student, way down the pecking order. In the 1990s, these caste equations did not play out explicitly. However, implicitly, I, from time to time, was accorded privileges that came not only from my urban, westernised otherness, but also from my caste status. These were teachers of a traditional form living traditional lives. One teacher, for example, walked in public spaces with his wife keeping seven paces behind him. For me, a historic moment of my personal journey in unpacking my caste consciousness came during *urizhcil* as my oiled body lay on the ground and was massaged by a teacher's foot. To allow one's adult body to lie vulnerable on the ground and be massaged by another man's (my teacher's) foot is, in itself, a difficult and fearful business. Add to this, the hidden emotions of caste identity and conflict. These prejudices and fears run deep and need a separate research exercise, but, for the moment, my lived experi-ence is shared, to reflect on the *nambudiri nair* interrelationship in Kottayyam Thampuran's plays.

The four plays are all set in the liminal, asocial space of the forest rather than when the Pandavas were peacefully living in the palace or during the great war when the two sets of cousins were bent on killing each other. Instead, the Pandavas heroes are either escaping from the Kauravas or banished to live like ascetics or *sanyasis*. This liminal space helps Kottayam Thampuran renegotiate the inter-relationships between *nairs* and *nambudiris* with the *nambudiri brahmins* play-ing a subordinate role to the *kshatriya nairs*, and the dramas all culminate in the liminal act, the death of the social antagonist the demon(s), almost as a sacrificial dead body to the holy flame of performance. Zarrilli's *Kathakali Dance Drama*

(2000a) is subtitled *Where Gods and Demons Come to Play* but might be more apt as "Where Demons Come to Die"!

David Bolland's *A Guide to Kathakali* (1980) gives the details on these deaths, which are summarised here: (1) in *Kalyana Saugandhikam* ("The Flower of Good Fortune"), perhaps the least bloody of all plays, Bhīma kills Krodhavasa, who guards the lake of the Saugandhika flowers (33–34); (2) in *Baka Vadha* ("Death of Baka"), Bhīma kills two demons – his wife's brother, Hidamba, and then Baka (22–24); (3) in *Kirmira Vadha* ("Death of Kirmira") Arjuna kills the demon Sardula and Bhīma kills the demon King Kirmira after a fierce fight (27–28); (4) in *Kalakeya Vadha* ("Death of Kalekeya"), Arjuna fights and kills the *asuras* (demons) Vajraketu and Vajrabahu and later kills two more *asuras*, Nivatakavacha (who lives under the sea) and Kalakeya (who has been attacking *devaloka* [heaven]) (31–32).

Within the liminal existence of the *pandavas* in the forest, these demons may be understood as enemy tribal chiefs, the dangerous other of peaceful meditating ascetics, like Hanuman in "The Flower of Good Fortune." In establishing the threat to the socioeconomic interests of the settled caste world from the outside, the relationship between the caste world and the tribal world is very precisely delineated by Guha in describing what he terms as the "the persistent tribes" (2013:56–64). As Guha points out, while the settled agrarian caste order evolved out of tribal existence, tribes not only pre-dated the settled agrarian world, but also continued to respond to it, negotiating, and existing for the caste Hindu social order as an external enemy. The social space of the caste order needed constant protection from tribal identification and territorial threat.

In Kathakali dramas, this theme of the killing of the demonic anti-social/tribal enemy celebrates the power of the *nair* warrior and is a common motif right across the repertoire of 36 plays whose stories and list of characters are available in a collection by David Bolland (1980). Nine of these plays include killing/death (*vadha*) in the title and in a number of others the words for war (*yudha*) or victory (*vijaya*). Of such playful killings, Schechner's observation is relevant:

> This kind of playing at killing emphasizes individual or small group action and teamwork. It is scripted behavior. In time, playing/hunting may generate the symbolic activities of ritual and drama. This transformation may be a function of what Lorenz calls "displacement activity": when two conflicting impulses prevent each other from being activated a third action results. In animals, displacement activity is often ritualised behavior. In humans, the conflicting impulses may be the wish to hunt people versus love bonds for members of one's own species, culture or kin group. The displacement activity is a ritual or drama in which humans kill humans – but only "in play".

> (1988:108–109)

What then are the two conflicting impulses that are displaced creating the playful Kathakali dancing warrior? Kathakali developed in the seventeenth century during a time of relative peace, which allowed the king to redirect the warring energies of his *nair* soldiers internally, towards policing his own people. With Kathakali came the contradictory tasks of both controlling and entertaining them. The *nair* warrior performers subdue and yet enchant via the image of the dancing warrior who playfully threatens and entertains. The warrior's training in acts of embodied aggression is translated into theatrical gestures on the Kathakali stage. His real ability to threaten, punish and kill is woven into the thematic, choreo-graphic and performance structures of Kottayam Thampuran's four plays. This indeed is now a flamboyant celebration of *nair* caste domination.

In these four plays by Kottayam Thamburan, the central characters are the epic heroes of the *Mahabharata*: Bhīma in *Baka Vadha* and *Kalyana Saugandhika*, Yudhishthira/Dharmaputra in *Kirmira Vadha* and Arjuna in *Kalakeya Vadha*. These four stories minimise religious structures and the role of the gods and enhance the role of the *nair* warrior.

The first drama, *Baka Vadha*, has the five Pandava brothers, *kshatriya* warriors like the *nairs*, protecting a *brahmin* family from a monster, Baka, whom Bhīma kills. Even in the liminal space of the forest, interrelationships are important: Bhīma kills another asocial demon, Hidimba, but marries his sister, the demoness Hidimbi. Bhīma here is a warrior and a king, killing off the enemy while expand-ing territory through marrying the enemy's sister.

The second play, *Kirmira Vadha*, has a thousand *brahmins* waiting to be fed, with Draupadi, the Pandava consort, left with no food in her cooking vessel. She prays directly to Krishna, needing no *brahmin* intermediary or any Vedic ritual. Krishna appears before Draupadi and solves her problem. Separate from this epi-sode is the killing of demon Kirimira, a cousin of Baka in the previous story.

In the third story, *Kalakeya Vadha*, Arjuna goes to heaven to meet his father Indra, and by this demonstrates a direct link between the *kshatriyas* and the gods. No intermediary *brahmins* are needed to get to heaven. He then serves his father by killing four demons – Vajraketu, Vajrabahu, Nivatakavach and Kalakeya.

The fourth story, *Kalyana Saugandhikam*, is the only one of the four plays not titled after the killing of a demon. In this story, the hero is Hanuman, a monkey who is also a half-brother of Bhīma, as both are born of Vayu, the god of wind. When Bhīma confronts Hanuman, a devotee of Rama, Hanuman does not ini-tially have a divine form/status. Bhīma calls upon Hanuman to reveal this divine form and then, as Hanuman obliges, the *kshatriya/nair* Bhīma is linked directly to Hanuman's divine form. By these thematic choices, the *nairs* in at least three of the four plays have a direct access to god (Krishna in *Kirmira Vadha*, Indra in *Kalkeya Vadha*, and Hanuman, son of Vayu, in *Kalyana Saugandhikam*). The *brahmins* are there to be protected and fed, but have no agency and exercise no ritual power in the plays. Thematically, these stories are moving away from the religio-temple hegemony of the *brahmin nambudiris*. In Kottayyam Thampuran's dramas, it is the *nair* dancing warrior who is at the centre of his universe. This includes that inherent ability to threaten and frighten. To maintain social order, this power also needs to be reined in, as it is done in "The Flower of Good Fortune," with the ascetic Hanuman teaching Bhīma a lesson of humility.

The episode of Bhīma's humiliation by Hanuman may be conceptually perceived as highlighting the untouchable view of the caste order as critiqued through the ascetic or *sanyasi*. Once again I reiterate that this section is being explored conceptually, working with structural categories of Hindu thought, and not empirically. Hanuman here is conceptually an ascetic, living in the forest. His meditation is violated by Bhīma in search of flowers for Draupadi. To teach Bhīma a lesson, Hanuman the ascetic transforms himself into an old and dying monkey and lies down in the path of the aggressive Bhīma. He lies down on the left side of the stage denoting his lower status. By this, Hanuman, it may be argued, takes on the untouchable's place, and point of view, in the caste order. The ascetic is transformed into an old monkey that may be perceived materially as a dying carcass, and Bhīma must consequently become a remover of the near dead. The impurity associated with removal of dead animals pollutes a caste permanently, making them untouchable. By touching the dead animal, they are deemed permanently polluted. Bhīma therefore refuses to touch the impure monkey and instead tries to lift Hanuman's tail by using his club. In failing to lift Hanuman's tail, Bhīma is humbled and controlled. On Bhīma's request, the ascetic Hanuman, having critiqued Bhīma's caste arrogance, reveals his divine self. After this lesson in humility from Hanuman, Bhīma kills Krodhavas, the monster guarding the grove of flowers. In the context of the real world, the *nair* warrior Bhīma, having been controlled by the divine Hanuman, returns to exercising his rights and responsibilities as accorded to him by his king to whom the *nair* owed loyalty unto death. The *nair* warrior works to keep the social weave in order.

Untouchability and the caste-based social weave

In documenting Kerala's caste hierarchies, Zarrilli notes a tripartite division of non-polluting high castes, higher polluting castes and lower polluting castes (Zarrilli 2000a:21). Within the "touchable life" of the higher castes, the higher polluting lower castes are allowed into the no-touch space of the village while the lower polluting castes are kept out. Gough and Schneider (1961) offer a specific detailing of the caste structure as well as the laws of untouchability and pollution. From their research (312–313), one can conclude the absence from Kathakali audiences of at least those highly polluting castes like the *pulyas* and *parayas* that lived outside of the village and had strict taboos: "As highly polluting castes, Pulyas and Parayas were theoretically forbidden to approach the high castes within a distance of sixty-four feet. They might not enter the 'good' area of the village or walk on the main paths" (313). Similarly, Robin Jeffrey's research uncovers the following order:

> a Nair can approach but not touch a Namboodiri Brahmin: a Chovan [Ezhava] must remain thirty-six paces off, and a Pulayan slave ninety-six steps distant. A Chovan must remain twelve steps away from a Nair, and a Pulayan sixty-six steps off, and a Parayan some distance farther still. Pulayans and

Parayars, who are the lowest of all, can approach but not touch, much less may they eat with each other.

(1976:9–10)

Thus, set out above, and increasingly over the centuries, this was the texture of the social body watching a Kathakali performance as it was performed in a temple, at a landlord's home or in the village square.

In such a social world, the onstage ritualisation of the attack or retreat impulse choreographed with the alternating theme of war and peace resonated with the soldier's warring impulse in the kingdom. With socioeconomic existence in medieval Kerala divided into a series of little kingdoms, war was the central business of survival; authority was hierarchised with divisions existing right down into and within the "polluting" lower castes. In such an intensely intimate and divided world, order had to be maintained. From the highest of the high to the lowest of the low, each individual being had to keep, and to be kept in their place. The system had to warn and instil a fear of transgression, forging the base of Kathakali's gestures of embodied aggression.

Seen in the context of the seventeenth-century sword-carrying *nair* soldiers-turned-performers, with real rights to dominate and subjugate, the following playful dialogue between Bhīma and Hanuman takes on a threatening tone. By way of illustration, the following passage, recited from memory, is from the Kathakali text "The Flower of Good Fortune," followed by my own translation into English.

Vazhiyil ninnu poka vaikathey vanaradhama Pokaykil nine
Muzhutta kopamodaduthu njan ninte Kazhuttil unpotu pitichudan
Thazhacha ninney erinju njan ee vazhikku povathinanakulam

(Get out the way you lowest amongst monkeys, get out. My rage increases, I will grab you by your neck and beat you, you fat monkey. I will throw you far, get out of the way you lowest among monkeys.)

The phrase "lowest among monkeys" is Bhīma the warrior's interpretation of the situation. There is nothing on stage, or in the appearance or costuming of the monkey that would suggest that he is the lowest. Bhīma's scorn and derision are his interpretation. Bhīma the warrior's contempt for lower life belongs not just to the story but also to the values embedded at the heart of the caste system, an upper-caste *nair*'s contempt for the lower castes. On stage, this contempt is expressed through a violent expression of disgust. The hands form into a fist through the hand gesture *mushti* and are raised to meet at the centre of the forehead. The face transforms into a specific expression of *vibhats* or disgust. Then the hands are smashed down to waist level, palms facing downward. It feels as if something is being thrown, beaten down, kept away violently. The face is contorted, with the expression suggesting the smelling of something disgusting, terrible, revolting.

How would the lower-caste world of *nair* funeral priests, barbers, washermen and a host of undefined others receive this message? The *nair* warrior's threat is flamboyant, violent and real, establishing his social dominance. Bhīma's dancing throughout this entire dialogue is aggressive and violent. He stands over the monkey threatening ironically to touch, beat him. He exaggerates his own superior position within the hierarchy while lowering the monkey to the lowest of the low. For the duration of this dialogue, the consequences of this encounter would appear very clearly to the lower-caste audience. If they were to block the path of the warrior, it could result in their death, as this early sixteenth-century account records.

> These [nayrs] live outside the towns, separate from other people, on their estates, which are fenced in. They have there all that they require; they do not drink wine. When they go anywhere they shout to the peasants that they may get out of the way where they have to pass; and the peasants do so, and if they did not do it the [nayrs] might kill them without penalty.
>
> (Barbosa 2010:129)

In this story, Bhīma ends up blocking his own journey, preventing him from easily hopping over the monkey's tail. This existential choice and freedom, of finding the easiest way forward, is not available to him. His free action is held back by a complex web of caste roles, interrelationships and obligations. In the caste system, even the powerful warrior dancers have their limits and may not transgress. Their gestures of embodied aggression must remain as gestures and not turn real and destructive.

Conclusion

This chapter sets up a theoretical framework using the debates in the social sciences around the values and structure of the caste system. While focusing on the role and function of the *nair* caste that first performed Kathakali in the seventeenth century, reference is made to texts of four Kathakali classics written by Kottayam Thamburan with greater attention to "The Flower of Good Fortune." The real caste equation between the ruler Kottayam Thampuran, the warrior *nair* community and the dominating *nambudiri brahmin* caste helps frame an understanding of the inter-caste relations setting up the performing power of the *nair* performer and his impact on his lower-caste audience. Using phenomenological, ethnographic and auto-ethnographic tools, the researcher has attempted to pry open the issue of caste and untouchability that has previously been neglected. This inquiry sets up a questioning of the traditional practice of Kathakali students touching the teacher's/*guru*'s feet, reflective of issues concerning the hierarchical inequalities of the caste order. This social context is necessary to explore the social weave that Kathakali drama and text is woven from and into. Out of this weave emerges its gestures of embodied aggression that are of value to the western contemporary performer as they work to draw out the psychophysical processes into the social, as will be evidenced in the next chapter, by the process of Helen and Peter performing Kathakali.

7   Performing Kathakali in Australia

The 22-month exercise of working one-on-one with Helen Smith and Peter Fraser offered valuable insights into both training, and performing Kathakali. Besides working on a few foundational Kathakali actor-training scenes and with an acknowledgement of the limitations on hand which included the difficulty of communicating precisely the complexity of the social/caste-related aspects of the texts, and with the additional complication of learning and performing plays written in a mix of Malayalam and Sanskrit, and knowing both Helen and Peter's interest in Shakespeare, I worked with them using elements of my creation of *The Magic Hour* (Loomba 2005; Calbi 2011) wherein I broke form with traditional Kathakali storytelling, and used scenes from William Shakespeare's *Othello* as a more direct path to Kathakali performativity. *The Magic Hour* includes Shakespearean texts translated into traditional Kathakali *padams* or songs, and scenes of high drama, like the famous murder sequence in *Othello*, Act V Scene II, which is enacted using the Kathakali form. *The Magic Hour* is in part inspired by a very successful *Othello in Kathakali* created by Sadanam Balakrishnan (Balakrishnan 2005:261–267).

As evidenced by Helen and Peter's engagement, in comparison with traditional Kathakali texts in *malayalam* and Sanskrit, Shakespearean texts in the English language and selected scenes from Shakespeare's *Othello* adapted into, and enacted through the Kathakali form, offer the western performer a more direct access to Kathakali performativity, including its gestures of embodied aggression. These gestures of embodied aggression offer a specific aesthetic value for intercultural performer training in Australia. These gestures draw the psychophysically absorbed and introverted performer out of themselves, and into the sociopsychophysical and celebratory mode of Kathakali performance. This sociopsychophysical performance brings the western performer into Kathakali's very particular offering of aesthetic pleasure or *rasa*.

Adapting the traditional training curriculum

Kathakali actor training entails working on both embodied dance practices, as well as dramatic texts and stories. This first section examines Kathakali's training practices, and the adaptions made to them. While a traditional training programme runs for six to eight years, an adapted programme for the new actor/performer training in Australia needs to make choices in terms of the lesser time available for western actor training. Adaptions needed to be made to the traditional dramatic texts, in response to certain difficulties faced by western learners as evidenced from working with Helen and Peter. This section details those difficulties faced and records the alternatives offered.

In a traditional Kathakali learning programme, each learning session begins with the *kumbital*, the formal Kathakali salutation. Traditionally, there are five salutations to be done, one to each corner (wherein resides the appropriate deity) and one to the lamp or to the centre where the *guru* is seated. Throughout the one-on-one training with Helen and Peter, while this formal salutation was done a few times, on most occasions each session began with just the one directed towards the centre, where I sat.

Following the salutation, we would begin the work with *meyyarappu* or body control exercises (Zarrilli 1984:104–138). These exercises are a modified form of *kalaripayattu*. Performed in sequence, these exercises create a choreography of their own. While there are a number of shorter connecting exercises, a few of the more challenging ones as described by Balakrishnan are detailed here.

Kaalatavu – stepping forward and kicking the right leg to the palm of the right hand which is stretched above the head, and then repeated with the left leg. The exercise is repeated 11 times in various ways. *Vechchiruttal* – sitting on one leg with the other extended, the body twists from one side to the other. *Thirichukuthal* – from a sitting position, rotating the arms backwards, forming a bridge, then continue the rotation to the original position, repeated three times each (101).

Helen and Peter performed *meyyarappu* with me in Australia, and then again in India with Pillai. These exercises are not done to formal *taalam* or rhythm and therefore posed no challenge to either Helen or Peter. They were both able to master them and take pleasure working them. These are also the set of exercises that Zarrilli mastered in the six months he worked on Kathakali actor training. This exercise routine inspired him to work on their source form *kalaripayattu* for the next seven years.

After these body exercises, Helen and Peter would work on their basic posture for increasing lengths of time. This involves learning to relax and be still, while sensing and working on their body both from within and from without.

Work on the basic posture was followed by *kannu sadhakam*, or eye exercises, and *cuzhippu*, or eye and hand co-ordination (Balakrishnan 2005:99). The eyes were exercised moving horizontally, from left to right and then from right to left, vertically from top to bottom and then the other way, diagonally from a top corner to an opposite bottom corner and then in figures of eight. These eye exercises were followed by synchronised movements of the eyes, hands and body. The co-ordination creates grace in the movements and links the body to the subjective self. The body begins to work as an integrated whole, and a sense of communing with oneself gives this exercise a spiritual feeling. Both Helen and Peter were able to master these exercises and get pleasure out of performing them.

The eye and hands would be followed by *Kaalsadhakam*, the practice of the basic four steps. These steps require the performer to chant along the spoken rhythm or *vaitari*. The teacher controls the tempo rhythm, moving the learner from slow, to medium, to fast and then finally, very fast. Both Helen and Peter enjoyed working on these basic steps. Over time, they were able to master these steps and own them.

In the traditional training programme, two choreographed dance routines follow these initial exercises. The first is the *todayyam*, and the second is the *purupaddu*. The *todayyam* is a dance sequence danced to all seven *talas* or rhythms in Kathakali. While this is a foundational dance training routine, the difficulties of intercultural actor training began here, with the complication of the *tala* added to the steps. With the difficulties faced working with Kathakali rhythm, each set of steps or phrase was taking far too long to master, especially the interconnecting *kalaashams*, which are like commas and full stops. While I had planned to finish the *todayyam* by the first three months of the one-on-one work, by the end of the first month I realised the need to adapt. I chose not to finish the *todayyam* and instead worked on more formal *kalaashams* primarily set to two *taalams*, *chemba* and *chembata*. By this choice, I was letting go of learning an intricately choreographed dance piece that runs for 25 minutes and instead worked on short, two- to three-minute dance choreographies, while keeping the *taal*/rhythm challenge to a minimum.

While in India, Pillai concentrated on teaching Helen and Peter the *purupaddu*. Helen did extremely well and in ten days finished learning the *purupaddu*. Peter, on the other hand, had a very difficult time. *Purupaddu* has dance choreography that moves from a slow tempo initially to a very fast tempo by the end. While the *todayyam* is never performed on stage, the *purupaddu* is an invocatory dance performed on stage in the *veisham* or costume of Krishna, with a headdress or *krishnamudi*. The dance has a lot of circular and ornamented moves, making the body bend as well as leap, to teach the student how to balance and manage the costume. Compared to the *todayyam*, it sets up a greater challenge and Peter was always struggling with it. This was in part due to Pillai's inability to offer one-on-one sessions as he had too many students to teach. At the end of ten days, they had both performed it with live musicians, a *chenda* and a *maddalam* player. Both Helen and Peter, despite the struggles, returned to Australia with a far greater ease of moving the body to rhythm.

In the initial learning period, a significant amount of time was spent in learning *mudras* or hand gestures (Balakrishnan 2005:135). It was surprising to note how difficult the two-handed gestures were to learn, i.e., those which had different *mudras* for each hand. For this part of the training, self-created home videos, recording hand gestures to a sentence, were emailed to the performers. It was easier to perform *mudras* to a sentence in English; the complications of the Kathakali text being in a mix of *malayalam* and Sanskrit, in a language they did not understand, made learning *mudras* to Kathakali *padams* or songs an extremely difficult exercise. It was here that a shift from traditional texts to Shakespeare was effected. Instead of struggling with the difficult Kathakali texts, audio recordings in the researcher's voice, of Iago, Othello and Desdemona's texts were made available. Appropriate *mudras* were identified for the words of the text, and Helen and Peter performed them to the audio tracks. These interventions proved very effective, as not only was the word more accessible, but the emotion and context too were played out through the language of gestures. With the Shakespearean text, the language of gestures stepped away from its exotic otherness, turning into what it is, a dramatic language carrying words, thoughts, feelings and emotions to an audience. The success with the hand gestures further encouraged me to work with Helen and Peter on the Kathakali scenes of Othello from *The Magic Hour*. This was developed later for a public performance at La Mama Theatre in Melbourne in June, 2016.

This entire process of learning led to their being ready to integrate the foot, hand and face movements into a complex choreography and danced enactment, bringing them to learn a set piece known as *shauryaguna*. In traditional Kathakali training, this danced dialogue *shauryaguna* is a set piece that integrates all elements of the Kathakali performer's skill. This particular set piece is from the Kathakali play "The Flower of Good Fortune" and features Bhīma asking for the permission of King Yudhishthira, his elder brother, to go and fight his enemy Dussassanna. It opens with the lowering of the curtain, revealing Bhīma the warrior. Bhīma openly displays his *bhava* of anger and acts aggressively with his gestures, postures and embodiment. Helen and Peter responded to these gestures of anger and aggression far more pleasurably than a scene of Bhīma in love in which he offers to get flowers for his beloved wife Draupadi. The male-centric Kathakali depiction of love and desire sat uneasily on both Helen and Peter's vision of love as a more equal thing, between lovers. Peter acknowledged that with love and desire he felt he was only mimicking the externals, while in the scene of anger and disgust, he felt he was more involved emotionally, from the inside.

In the first public performance that we danced *shauryaguna* together I led Helen and Peter through the set piece. As a leader, I was extra careful in making sure I was taking them along, helping them to arrive correctly at each end point of a rhythm cycle. This was done by my controlling my own embodied emotional state and by not allowing the *bhava* to rise within myself. By being emotionally stable, I was able to concentrate on keeping the precise *taalam* which, in a performance of more intense emotional embodiment, gets more complex. When possessed by the *bhava*, the performer tends to ride through individual markers of rhythm, and not acknowledge them as formally and precisely as in rehearsal. Later, in a solo Kathakali piece by me, Helen and Peter were able to see the same piece done more flamboyantly.

We also worked regularly on *rasaabhinaya*, or the training of the nine *bhavas* or basic emotions. This took place in two stages. In the first, I would just work the face, with each emotion being located at a specific area or muscle; for example, *shringar* or desire in the eyebrows, *raudra* or anger in the cheeks, *vibhats* or disgust in the nose and *bhaya* or fear in the eyes. To take the concentration away from the face and to embody the emotional state, I would then have them work through the *bhavas* using my own playful creation, which relies on archetypes of birds and animals. For example, they would express "desire like a peacock, anger like a lion, fear like a deer, pride like an elephant, wonder like an owl, sadness like a fish, and disgust like a vulture."

While the *Natyashastra* details only eight emotions, in Kathakali practice there are nine, as the last emotion, *shantam* or peace, is the cessation of the act of emoting.

At the end of this traditional training work, Helen and Peter were ready for performing and sharing the work with a Melbourne audience. Kathakali's sociopsychophysical actor training completes and realises itself when it is brought into the social space of a performance. The performers needed to perform to make sense of their training. A choice of performance pieces, choreographies and texts had now to be made. Explaining to Helen and Peter traditional Kathakali stories and texts set up issues of intercultural translation. A mentalist engagement was needed, in translating theory to practice, in interpreting traditional Kathakali texts for performance, in contextualising for Helen and Peter the archetypical characters in terms of their social and historic location. This required explanations about text and culture, explaining and answering all their questions about the caste system, social relationships and existential conditions within the old social. This then became a very mentalist, textual exercise.

While acknowledging, as a problem, this area of translating texts of the old social for performers in the new social, and recognising it as a separate area of research, I chose instead to work with scenes from Shakespeare adapted to the Kathakali form, in what was felt by Helen and Peter as a more direct route to experiencing Kathakali's pedagogy and embodied performativity. While staying with a traditional Kathakali opening piece *thiranoku* for the performance, scenes from *The Magic Hour* were selected by the three of us, for the more dramatic sections of the work. These scenes were Kathakali adaptions of Shakespeare's scenes. A familiarity with Shakespeare's characters Othello and Iago, as well as accompanying audio recordings of Shakespeare texts helped facilitate, for the performers, a more direct access to Kathakali performativity.

The first piece of a traditional performance is the *thiranoku*, the traditional curtain entry of a character. In a traditional performance, before the enactment of a scene the character is revealed briefly with the lowering and raising of the curtain. This action draws the audience's attention into the performance space and onto the character's presence. I worked to craft both Peter and Helen's *thiranoku*. Each character in their own *thiranoku* displayed a specific *bhava* or embodied emotional state. In Peter's *thiranoku* in which he played Iago, the stable emotion or *sthayi bhava* he was embodying was *vibhats* or disgust at having to serve Othello. As can be seen in the image below, in Helen's *thiranoku*, where she played Othello, the *sthayi bhava* was *raudra* or rage (Figure 7.1).

Helen and Peter in the *thiranoku* developed a stillness, a boldness, an openness and a presence that had come from their Kathakali training. This shift from the introverted psychophysicality of their individual creations described previously, to an extroverted sociopsychophysicality helped create what Barba frames as an eastern actor's "scenic presence" (Barba 1995:9). In Kathakali acting, this "scenic presence" emerges from the performer's comfort at observing, and at the same time being observed by an audience. This is what the Kathakali learner does every day of his learning life. The learner observes the teacher's demonstration, then acts and allows the teacher to observe and correct his or her own actions. This is what the performer needs to do in a *thiranoku*; to feel comfortable, boldly

Figure 7.1 Othello (Helen) Thiranoku (curtain entry) displaying a wounded rage (*raudra*).
(Photo courtesy of Darren Gill.)

observing an audience, as well as to be at ease at being observed by them. This
two-way process of observation is the core methodology of the mirroring process
of Kathakali learning, as argued throughout this book. The two *thiranokus* were
performed by Helen and Peter after 22 months of Kathakali training. The *thiranoku*, while seeming simple to perform, requires refined skills, especially moving
the eyes to the Kathakali rhythm or *talaam* as the audience sees most spectacu-
larly at the end of the sequence. Moving the eyes to Kathakali rhythm requires a
level of skill and ability that takes time to acquire. The next section documents
and analyses the creative interventions made through the vehicle of *The Magic
Hour*, working to perform Kathakali and Shakespeare in the new social.

The Magic Hour and the innercultural practice of performing Kathakali in Australia

This particular original construct of the innercultural is a response to the inadequacy
I feel towards the intercultural as a descriptive for my work in *The Magic Hour*.
This creation has been my very personal, individual project for the past 17 years
(read Loomba 2005:134–136). It works with both texts of Shakespeare and scenes
of Kathakali. The intercultural descriptive suggests the presence of separate cultures
outside of the performer, and separated from each other (Pavis 1996; Schechner
1990; Watson 2002). In contrast to the intercultural is the "intracultural" (Bharucha
2000; Landon-Smith 2016) which reacts to the intercultural with an offer of cultures

existing within a shared time and space – a shared geographic and cultural region. As a post-colonial Indian who read Shakespeare in school,[1] my performance of Shakespeare has no geographic or regional boundaries. My interest in Shakespeare's work exists as much within me as without. Both the intercultural and intracultural felt inadequate as definers of my experience with *The Magic Hour*. The innercultural is constructed as a response to both the intercultural and the intracultural. The innercultural reflect all cultures separated outside of me, but now existing within me, as part of me. As a post-colonial Indian with a historical relationship to the English language, and a conscious journey to Kathakali acting, my work with both forms of theatre emerges from my individual performative being. Both my work with Shakespeare and Kathakali come from within me as much as from without.

In a similar process, I respect Helen and Peter's work with other cultures and performative practices which have, through their hard work and dedication, been absorbed into their being, and exist in their bodies as one. For me, they had worked hard enough and long enough at Kathakali actor training for 22 months, for the culture of Kathakali too to be considered a part of their creative being. As for the plays of Shakespeare they already existed within their inner worlds and imagination.

With Helen, embedded into her performative being, along with her recent work with Kathakali, was her earlier work with Butoh. Both these forms embedded a contrary set of techniques into her body. Butoh gave her, for example, techniques and habits of breaking the body while with Kathakali she was able to create and hold the body in form, through formal gestures. In performing Othello's breakdown and rage to traditional Kathakali music, her body responded with a well-integrated set of gestures, both of the broken, as well as of the formal body. This cohabitation of Shakespeare, Butoh and Kathakali within her performative being expressed itself in the form of a very individual innercultural performance (Figure 7.2).

In similar mode, Peter's body inhabited a diversity of performative cultures, techniques and habits. When performing Iago, after months of Kathakali training to lower and ground his body, Peter returned to the very upward stance of a Venetian courtier, he was playing out both his Anglo-Saxon body habits as well as his acquired Kathakali training. These two cultures within one body created an attractive tension and presence. While working hard at form, rhythm and *taalam* through the entire length of the Kathakali training, when Peter finally came to embody Iago and express his evil, he used his BodyWeather training to imbue Iago's body, and the atmosphere around it, with a dark feeling of evil. Eventually, when he danced Kathakali displaying Iago's disgust at Othello, he returned to a form of mimicry, and eccentric exaggeration of the formal, which did, in the context of Iago's particular circumstance of having to serve a black man, express a precise feeling of *vibhats* or disgust (Figure 7.3).

---

1 Shakespeare in Asia is a significant area of scholarship. Asian practitioners have responded to Shakespeare's works for reasons as varied as talking back to empire, celebrating intercultural theatre, and negotiating identity in a multicultural world. For a glimpse into what is now an extensive field of scholarship, read Lan Li and Kennedy (2010) and William Peterson's interview with Ong Ken Sen (2014).

Figure 7.2 Othello (Helen Smith) threatening to murder a sleeping Desdemona (Lillian Warrum).

Figure 7.3 Iago's (Peter) disgust (*vibhats*) at serving Othello. (Photo courtesy of Darren Gill.)

Figure 7.4 Iago' jealousy and hate of Othello: An innercultural performance. (Photo courtesy of Darren Gill.)

By these examples, Helen and Peter were both, individually and through an appreciation of the innercultural, able to both absorb their Kathakali training and use it meaningfully in performance. The innercultural then lies within one individual body, and its creative expression. It lies as much within, as without. While it makes sense for the traditional Kathakali actor-training programme to exclude the non-traditional learner's own journey/culture/experience, and to stay within the rigours of the form, an innercultural exercise offers the opportunity to integrate the learner's previous experience, ability, culture and background into the process of working with the newly acquired culture. It is with this framework that Helen and Peter were encouraged to bring their own practices into the Kathakali performance space (Figure 7.4).

Performing Kathakali's gestures of embodied aggression

In this concluding section, I will describe and consider Helen and Peter's performance work in the context of Kathakali's gestures of embodied aggression. For each performer, I will analyse in greater detail a scene discussed in the previous section. The scenes were specifically selected for each performer to encourage the extroverted outward social display of gestures, and for them to experience the pleasure of performing Kathakali's gestures of embodied aggressions. These gestures in both the scenes chosen for Helen and Peter are performed to rhythm and when the performer embodies both the form and the rhythm, a performative power and pleasure or *rasa* is experienced. These gestures were first demonstrated by me and observed by both of them. Once absorbed, they were then free to make of them, through their innercultural practices, very individualised expressions and performances.

We selected the Othello murder scene for Helen, so she would be encouraged to take pleasure in these gestures of embodied aggression, to be bold, open and social, both with the formal embodied emotions or *bhava*, and her actions. During the course of this performance, while sitting in the green room and making up, she reflected on how pleasurable this process had been. The pleasure was of playing within the discipline of the *taalam* or rhythm structure, an emotion or *bhava*, openly, boldly, even flamboyantly. This pleasure may then be formally realised as *rasa*.

In performing the role of Othello, in the well-known Othello and Desdemona murder sequence in Act 5 Scene 2, Helen worked with her Butoh techniques and used Kathakali's embodied basic position, *bhavas* of rage and sadness, as well as a number of formal hand gestures. The Kathakali form helped add and layer an embodied form onto the formless/brokenness of her Butoh training. This tension between the formless and broken on the one hand (Butoh), and the formal and social on the other (Kathakali), helped create a delicate and refined tension.

Helen's playing of the murder sequence in Kathakali was worked through using Kathakali's gestures of embodied aggression. As evidenced in the previous chapter, these gestures of embodied aggression come from the *nair* warrior's social role in the seventeenth century. While these gestures of embodied aggression are directed toward the character on stage, they are simultaneously opened out and directed towards the social space of the performance. They demand boldness, an outwardly directed aggression, and an extroverted embodied presence bordering on flamboyance. These gestures draw a psychophysically absorbed performer out of the introverted experimental mode, into a more outward, extroverted and celebratory form of performance. What makes them not crude but sophisticated gestures of embodied aggression are the precise and complicated rhythms or *taalam* that accompany the scene. The performer is encouraged to explore a full-bodied flamboyance while performing within the sophisticated discipline of the rhythm structure or *taalam*.

The second scene that offered insights into Kathakali's embodied gestures was Peter's enactment of Iago, the scene where he gave his reasons for hating Othello. In the first part of the scene, Peter used hand gestures to enact Iago's monologue, corresponding with a recording of the speech in my voice. He then danced a Kathakali *padam* or song based on the same monologue. In the dance, he expresses his affections for Desdemona and his disgust and hate of Othello, whom he suspects of have slept with his wife Emilia. Peter displayed all the *bhavas* or emotions, openly and boldly, even squealing at one point with the delight of having planned the destruction of Othello's marriage.

In both Helen and Peter's scenes, the performers allowed themselves to be led by the rhythm, taking their embodied presence to its gestural limit while staying in touch with the rhythm, neither losing it, nor leading it, nor lagging too far behind it. When the rhythm is ridden with precision, a certain embodied power is available to the performer. In both these cases, the full-bodied possession of the rhythm or *taalam* brought these two performers to be possessed by what Barba frames as an "extra daily" energy. The performance, especially in Peter's case, seemed to step away at the end from a careful formal classical precision towards a wilder trance-like possessed state. Yet, the possession remained within the formal confines of the *taalam*, within the rhythm.

These gestures of embodied aggression and offerings of rhythm-driven states of possession are some of Kathakali's significant offerings for the contemporary performer. This making of one's own, of a formal dance theatre like Kathakali, within an innercultural exercise, is a very delicate task and requires the sustained intimacy of the one-on-one relationship to offer any hope of success.

In Helen and Peter's case, their work was well-appreciated by both audiences and critics, while Nithya Iyer's review in *Peril*, an online arts magazine, reflects an understanding of the context for the work which provides detailed, relevant descriptions of what the actors did:

> Among the most utterly arresting moments of the entire work is the scene where Helen Smith, embodying the mind of Othello, enters into a dance of death, demonstrating the fruits of her rich expertise in the controlled contortive nature of the Butoh form. Similarly, Peter Fraser, an exponent of the Bodyweather technique, is hauntingly present in his scenes as the jealous and crazed Iago. Both Smith and Fraser, currently learning Kathakali from Raina, are, in their own way, symbols of the changing tides of the Asian-Australian relationship, embodying the notion that these art forms are not religiously or culturally bound.
>
> (Iyer 2016)

The success of this innercultural work was not just critical, but more importantly through the pleasure experienced by all three, Helen, Peter and me. At the heart of this innercultural exercise was the joy or pleasure of performing the formal routines of Kathakali with its clarity of *bhavas* or emotional states, and its openly displayed gestures of embodied aggression that work to draw the psychophysically absorbed performer out of the introverted inward state to an outward, bold, celebratory sociopsychophysicality. This successful creative project was a result of a respect for the traditional mirroring methodology that was successfully translated in the Australian context through the sustained one-on-one work with the learners as well as the adaptations made through an acknowledgement of the work being done in its new location, in Australia.

8 Kathakali for the global performer and researcher

As a part of this concluding chapter I work with my Australian experience to deepen and widen an understanding of the sociopsychophysical in the context of twenty-first-century global performer training and research. With this objective in mind I reference Frank Camelli's *Performer Training Reconfigured: Post Psychophysical Perspectives for the Twenty-first Century* (2019), a reconfiguring of the psychophysical processes of performing training. While appreciating Camelli's exploration, through his "post psychophysical" framing of actor-training processes, I reiterate, as previously with Zarrilli's psychophysical, the centrality of the human relationship, that special creative bond of master and disciple, with all its consequent objective, subjective and inter-subjective implications.

As detailed in Chapter 3, an appreciation of the sociopsychophysical builds on the psychophysical traditions of western actor training initiated to mend the psycho physical/body mind split in western actors. During the course of this practice-led research, I saw at first hand, as it were, this mind/body split in the western learner, wherein the learner needed to engage mentally with an action before embodying it – a mental interpretation before an embodied communion. Camelli (2019) however critiques the psychophysical tradition, suggesting it as being human body-centric – a tradition that is primarily engaged with the actor's body/mind, neglecting the environment – the "sociomaterial" conditions of the stage or studio where the performance or rehearsal/training is happening. In the context of twenty-first-century actor training, from the previous human body/mind absorption of the psychophysical tradition he shifts the focus to the body/mind "interrelational" with the "sociomaterial," highlighting the actor's relationship with technology. This relationship he further explores as a post-phenomenology.

> Postphenomenology [Chapter 2] is the philosophical study of the structures of experience and consciousness. As formulated by Don Ihde and as used in this book, postphenomenology marks a hybrid form of phenomenology that combines classic phenomenology with pragmatism and *technoscience.*
>
> (Camelli 2019:220)

In Camelli's reconfiguration of performer training for the twenty-first century the trilogy of terms is the psychophysical, the post psychophysical and the post phenomenological. Camelli, working with the psychophysical as the springboard for the post psychophysical, notes that Zarrilli's anthropological /ethnographic scholarship develops an interest in embodiment and phenomenology, the change reflecting shifts in academic trends:

> A seminal chapter in Phillip B. Zarrilli's *Psychophysical Acting* (2009) titled "An Enactive Approach to Acting and Embodiment" is based very closely on an article that appeared a few years earlier under the heading of "Towards a Phenomenological Model of the Actor's Embodied Modes of Experience" (2004). The change in title reflects shifts in scholarly trends to update psychophysical discourse with contemporary developments.
>
> (Camelli 2019:57)

Even as he notes the change Camelli critiques Zarrilli, arguing that while he on the one hand does engage with twenty-first-century phenomenology, and explores processes beyond the body, his scholarship remains, on the other hand, primarily limited to an exploration of the experiences of the body. For Camelli, Zarrilli does not engage with the kind of "sociomaterial" space and technology in which Camelli is interested. Camellli's interest lies in the phenomenology of the body's experience of technology or in reverse, the phenomenology of technology's experience of the body. In that symbiotic relationship Cameilli argues is the genesis of post-phenomenology and its more direct connect with twenty-first-century performer training and scholarship.

At the outset I have no argument with Camelli. My point of departure, however, with both Zarrilli's interest in the psychophysical and phenomenological, and in Camelli's post psychophysical/postphenomenological, is not a disinterest in the individual performer's body/mind integration or in the relationship of the body/mind with technology, but instead a counter-interest in the joint action, the deep creative relationship of two human beings working together, with one (the *guru*) leading the other (the *shishya*) towards a common artistic objective.

The sociopsychophysicality of the *guru shishya* tradition, while existing in a seemingly conservative field of the "tradition seeking avante-garde" (Schechner 1990:347–350), simultaneously works to look forward and be more radical. I frame its "forward-looking" trajectory by tweaking Camelli's defence of the post psychophysical: "this is not to surrender the primacy of human action, but, pertinently, of a more distributed form of agency and intentionality" (2019:220). While retaining the "distributed form of agency and intentionality" I replace "human action" with the phrase "joint human action," locating the joint action further in the special conditions of one actor having mastered the action and the other in the mode of mastering that action. Similarly significant parts of Camelli's reconfiguring of the psychophysical for twenty-first-century actor training may work in terms of joint action. What works for Camelli's post psychophysical may then also work conceptually for the sociopsychophysical. My offer of the *guru shishya* holds potential then for a wider engagement with twenty-first-century actor training and research.

Guru shishya: new possibilities

There are, surprisingly for the author, few research publications that deal directly with the *guru shishya* tradition. While there are a number of studies done in the field of music, research on *guru shishya* in the space of embodied practices, dance and performance are limited. As documented in this book, those studies that do deal with the *guru shishya*, as in Dalidowizc's study of Kathak dance, concentrate more on the creativity of the *guru* and the innovations within the learning process. Straight down the middle studies of the embodied imitative process in master disciple learning are, surprisingly, an unexplored area. The studies that do engage with *guru shishya* more often than not use journalistic methods of interviewing *gurus* or writing their life stories. Research for this thesis suggests the reason for this is, in part, a lack of interest in the imitative methodology. In music, this imitative methodology is perceived differently. While a *tabla* learner may be seen to imitate her *guru*, she will not be said to be mimicking her *guru*. On the other hand, it is easier to have a Kathakali *guru* teaching facial expressions being perceived as teaching the art of mimicry. A rethink of the pedagogy of Kathakali actor training and a move from mimicry to mirroring are timely. Digging down into the particularities of the master–pupil relationship is a significant priority for current performer training and research. This book offers a successful case study to continue to develop such thinking.

One-on-on actor training

This book and its research successfully demonstrate the validity of the one-on-one mode of sociopsychophysical actor training through the central exercise of the master practitioner teaching two Australian performers. The establishment of a long-term one-on-one working relationship between teacher and learner, in an intercultural context, is then the primary success of this research exercise. This success opens up the possibility of one-on-one actor training being explored more rigorously in contemporary intercultural actor-training programmes. While the workshop mode of actor training is common practice and will continue to be the norm, an addition to each workshop of the one-on-one mode will further deepen the work of the teacher, master practitioner or workshop conductor.

Historiography of Kathakali performance

For contemporary intercultural actor training this book encourages the deepening of the historiographical knowledge of the practice. From traditional anthropology and ethnography, to historical and cultural studies, literature illumining the social weave of the Indian caste system, and its effect on Kathakali texts and performativity furthered the practice-led work with Helen and Peter. The research threw new light on the social experience of the caste system and untouchability, and this exercise helped highlight certain existential elements of Kathakali performativity. From the role of the *nair* community, and its interrelationships with other castes, and from an understanding of the civic role of the *nair* warriors, emerged a vision of Kathakali's gestures of embodied aggression. These gestures are an important offering to twenty-first-century actor training, drawing out as they do the psycho physically challenged and introverted western performer into the social space of performance. This book offers to the western/global performer the socially directed gestures of aggression that emerge out of an understanding of Kathakali's sociopsychophysicality. The author encourages the use of this particular framing, as a means to focus new research on Kathakali, as well as an offer for global performers to use it as a tool, a guide or a reference to deepen their engagement with Kathakali. While a contemporary/western/global performer working with a traditional master should respectfully allow the *guru* to lead for a length of time, once trust has been established, a recognition of the value of these gestures of embodied aggression, by both parties, will help select more engaging and effective text, scenes, roles and episodes. A raging *raudra* Bhīma threatening to drink Dushsanna's blood, an Othello moving to murder a Desdemona, a contemptuous Bhīma mocking an old monkey blocking the way, are more rewarding scenes to explore, than elaborately crafted and popular love scenes of Nala and Damayanti meeting in a garden or forest grove. Once the initial work with the form is done, which may take over a year of work, performing gestures of embodied aggression set to complex *taalams* or rhythms will engage, excite and reward the contemporary performer in equal measure. Of course, the traditional *guru* too has to come to the table as it were, and appreciate, as discussed previously, the difference of teaching in the intercultural context scenes of *raudra* or anger and *vibhats* or disgust, to those of the less accessible emotional states of *shringar* or desire and *hasya* or laughter. Once both master and pupil commune with the appropriate *bhava* then *rasa* shall follow.

Both these claims, of the values of representing Kathakali as a sociopsychophysical theatre, and of the master practitioner tasting aesthetic pleasure or *rasa*, coalesce to validate each other, and find a point of commonality in the act of mirroring. The act of mirroring is a nuanced and complex sociopsychophysical practice and an enriching site for a tasting of aesthetic pleasure or *rasa*. The latest research in neuroscience helped change the previously reductive narrative of mimicking, to a more nuanced and contemporary mirroring, setting up Kathakali actor training, and similar eastern sociopsychophysical forms, as sites for greater interdisciplinary research and exploration. This shift is not merely of semantic value, but instead offers the opportunity for the detailing of a complex process by which the brain observes and acts. From a realisation of the value of engaging with new scientific knowledge, the research in this book feeds successfully into the growing interdisciplinary field of neuroscience and performer training.

Archetype

A significant shift in perception for the researcher has been the move away from the exotic eye exercises that have been placed centrally in western narratives of Kathakali actor training, towards the more significant exercise of the basic posture. This basic posture engages the entire body, serves the archetype from within, like a scaffold does a building. At the International Centre for Kathakali, there are now 200 young women out of a body of 240 students, learning Kathakali. They play both male and female characters. This sets up exciting possibilities of women performers/feminine bodies scaffolding male, female, godly and animal archetypes. With certain institutions like the International Centre in New Delhi, and individual master practitioners opening up to teaching women, an opportunity exists now for women performers globally to engage more deeply with the art of Kathakali.

Kathakali abhinaya and Stanislavsky

Connected to the performer's ability to experience *rasa* first theorised in the *Natyashastra* are all the related concepts that drive the performer's imagination into a state of emotional embodiment. These individual concepts, which may be translated in English as "given circumstances," "action" and "emotion memory," all resonate with Konstantin Stanislavsky's work to create an actor's "inner emotional life." His later journey to a method of physical actions brings the Stanislavskian system closer to the Kathakali method, wherein the learner works at and learns a physical score, and through the physical arrives at the emotional and psychological. By this comparison, a new area of research lies in working to discover how what Stanislavsky did for the actor playing individual realistic naturalistic characters may converse with Kathakali's methods to create epic archetypical characters. *Rasa* theory may then talk, converse with the "Method."

Caste, untouchability and performativity

While connecting the lived experience of the caste system with Kathakali text and performativity, this book opens up another area of research linking the performer's body to its culture and performativity. An example of performativity's connection to the social practice of untouchability is the Kathakali performer's gaze, which often works on stage as an expression of domination, suggesting that when bodies cannot touch, power is exercised by staring, and not by touching. The celebrated Kathakali eye exercise has now a local context within the social practice of untouchability. By this example, the caste contextualisation of the performing arts informs the very texture of the body's performativity. Perhaps, if the hands touched more, the eyes would stare less? Caste, untouchability and performativity in the Indian arts are an exciting new area of research.

Finally, in a globalising world, the research opens up for practitioners engaging with sociopsychophysical forms like Kathakali the one-on-one space as a significant site for intercultural actor training. Today, most major cities around the world have available Asian practitioners of one form or another. For formal drama schools, this book works to open out an engagement of student actors with the Asian master performers available in their community. This engagement through a sustained one-on-one relationship, in addition to group workshops and classroom training in the drama class, is a new model of incorporating traditional eastern arts into drama training programmes. In actor-training institutions like drama schools and university drama departments, master practitioners are often invited to teach, in the workshop mode. This book presents an argument for students to be encouraged to build a relationship with individual master practitioners living and working locally, and sustain it through some part if not the entire length of the programme. As evidenced if the students were to meet the *guru*, while continuing with their institutional studies, in the *guru*'s home, even once or twice a week, over a length of time, their work would be enriched.

By these examples set out above, I suggest, this research exercise, set in Australia and India, has meaning and value for a global community of performers and researchers.

Bibliography

Antonin, A. *Collected Works Volume 1*. Translated by Victor Corti. Calder & Boyars Ltd, 1968.

———. *Selected Writings*. Edited by Susan Sontag. University of California Press, 1976.

Averill, J. R. "Emotions in Relation to Systems of Behaviours." In *Psychological and Biological Approaches to Emotion*, edited by Nancy L. Stern, Leventhal B.,Trabasso T., et al. Lawrence Erlbaum Associates, 1990, pp. 385–402.

Balakrishnan, S. *Kathakali: A Practitioner's Perspective*. Poorna Publications, 2005.

Barba, E. "Words or Presence." *The Drama Review*, 1972, Vol. 16, No. 2, pp. 47–54.

———. *The Million*, Video Artfilms digital (Firm). Originally released by Odin Teatret Film. Drama-Experimental Theater, 1979.

———. "The Fiction of Duality." *New Theatre Quarterly*, vol. 5, no. 20, 1989, pp. 311–314.

———. "The Steps on the River Bank." *The Drama Review*, vol. 38, no. 4, 1994, pp. 107–120.

———. *The Paper Canoe*. Routledge, 1995.

Barba, Eugenio, and Simonne Sanzenbach. "The Kathakali Theater." *The Tulane Drama Review*, vol. 11, no. 4, 1967, pp. 37–50.

Barba, Eugenio, and Phillip Zarrilli. "Eugenio Barba to Phillip Zarrilli: About the Visible and the Invisible in the Theatre and about ISTA in particular." *Theatre Drama Review*, vol. 32, no. 3, 1988, pp. 7–16.

Barbosa, Duarte. *The Book of Duarte Barbosa*. Translated by Mansel Longworth Dames. Asian Educational Services, 1989.

———. *A Description of the Coasts of East Africa and Malabar in the Beginning of the Sixteenth Century*. Translated by Henry E. J. Stanley. Ashgate Publishing Group, 2010.

Basham, L. A. *The Origin and Development of Classical Hinduism*. Oxford University Press, 1989.

Bharucha, R. *Theater and the World, Politics and Performance of Culture*. Routledge, 1993.

———. *The Politics of Cultural Practice: Thinking Through Theater in the Age of Globalization*. Wesleyan University Press, 2000.

Blair, Rhonda. "Cognitive Neuroscience and Acting: Imagination, Conceptual Blending, and Empathy." *Theater Drama Review*, vol. 53, no. 4, 1988, pp. 92–103.

———. *The Actor, Image, and Action: Acting and Cognitive Neuroscience*. Routledge, 2008.

Bolland, David. *A Guide to Kathakali*. National Book Trust, 1980.

Bolt, Barbara. "The Magic is in Handling." In *Practice as Research: Approaches to Creative Arts Enquiry*, edited by Estelle Barrett, and Barbara Bolt. I.B Tauris, 2007, pp. 27–34.

Borghi, A. M., and F. Cimatti. "Embodied Cognition and Beyond: Acting and Sensing the Body." *Neuropsychologia*, vol. 48, no. 3, 2010, pp. 763–73.

Bottini, G. "Feeling Touches in Someone Else's Hand." *Neuroreport*, vol. 13, 2002, pp. 249–252.

Bourdieu, Pierre. *The Logic of Practice*. Policy Press, 1990.

Bowers, Faubion. *Theatre in the East: A Survey of Asian Dance and Drama*. Grove Press, 1956.

Boyce-Tillman, June, et al. *PaR for the Course Issues Involved in the Development of Practice-Based Doctorates in the Performing Arts*. The Higher Education Academy. University of Winchester, 2012.

Brandon, James R. *Theatre in Southeast Asia*. Harvard University Press, 1967.

Brass, M., and C. Heyes. "Imitation: Is Cognitive Neuroscience Solving the Correspondence Problem?" *Trends in Cognitive Sciences*, vol. 9, no. 10, 2005, pp. 489–495.

Buchanan, Francis (Hamilton). *A Journey from Madras, Canara and Malabar*, vol. 2. Black, Perry and Kingsbury, 1807.

Calbi, Maurizio. "Postcolonial Entanglements: Performing Shakespeare and Kathakali in Ashish Avikunthak's *Dancing Othello*." *Anglistica*, vol. 15, no. 2, 2011, pp. 27–32.

Camelliri, Frank. *Performer Training Reconfigured: Post Psychophysical Perspectives for the Twenty-First Century*. Bloomsbury/Methuen Drama.

Chatterjee, Ananya. "Training in Indian Classical Dance: A Case Study." *Asian Theater Journal*, vol. 13, no. 1, 1996, pp. 68–91.

Chaudhury, P. J. "Catharsis in the Light of Indian Aesthetics." *Journal of Aesthetics and Art Criticism*, vol. XV, no. 2, 1956, pp. 218–226.

Coomaraswamy, A. K. *The Mirror of Gesture*. 3rd ed. Munshiram Manoharlal, 1957.

Craig, Edward Gordon. *The Mask*. Craus Reprint Corp, 1913.

Crossley, Nick. *Reflexive Embodiment in Contemporary Society*. Macgraw-Hill, Education, 2006.

Csordas, Thomas J. "Embodiment as a Paradigm." *Anthropology Ethos*, vol. 18, no. 1, 1990, pp. 5–47.

———. *Embodiment and Experience: The Existential Ground of Culture and Self*. Cambridge University Press, 1994.

———. "Embodiment and Cultural Phenomenology." In *Perspectives on Embodiment*, edited by Gail Weiss and Honi fern Haber. Routledge, 1999, pp. 143–162.

———. "Intersubjectivity and Intercorporeality." *Subjectivity*, vol. 22, 2008, pp. 110–121.

Cynkutis, Zbigniew. *Acting with Growtowski -Theater as a Field for Experiencing Life*. Translated by Khalid Tyabji. Routledge, 2015.

Dalidowicz, Monica. "Crafting Fidelity." *Journal of the Royal Anthropological Institute (N.S.)*, vol. 21, 2015, pp. 838–854.

Das, Veena. *Structure and Cognition: Aspects of Hindu Caste and Ritual*. Oxford University Press, 1977.

Daugherty, Diane, and Marlene Pitkow. "Who Wears the Skirts in Kathakali?" *The Drama Review*, vol. 35, no. 2, 1988, pp. 138–156.

de Zoete, Beryl, and Walter Spies. *Dance and Drama in Bali*. Faber and Faber, 1938.

Delgado, Maria M., and Paul Heritage, editors. *In Contact with the Gods: Directors Talk Theatre*. Manchester University Press, 1996.

Dumont, Louis. *Homo Hierarchicus: An Essay on the Caste System*. University of Chicago Press, 1970.

Ekman, P., and R. Davidson. *The Nature of Emotion, Fundamental Questions*. Oxford University Press, 1994.

Fitzgerald, Tim. "Review of 'Drama and Ritual in Early Hinduism by Natalia Lidova and Farley P. Richmond'." *Asian Folklore Studies*, vol. 55, no. 1, 1996, pp. 182–184.

Foley, Kathy. "Founders of the Field: South and South East Asia and Introduction." *Asian Theatre Journal*, vol 28, no. 2, 2011, pp. 437–442.

———. "John Emigh." *Asian Theatre Journal*, vol. 28, no. 2, 2011, pp. 451–462.

———. "Melvyn Helstien." *Asian Theatre Journal*, vol. 28, no. 2, 2011, pp. 443–450.

Fraser, Peter. *Personal Interview*. 30 June 2016.

Fuller, Zack. "Seeds of an Anti-Hierarchic Ideal: Summer Training at Body Weather Farm." *Theatre, Dance and Performance Training*, vol. 5, no. 2, 2014, pp. 197–203, 2013.

Gabriele, Alex. "A Sense of Belonging and Exclusion: 'Touchability' and 'Untouchability' in Tamil Nadu." *Ethnos*, vol. 73, no. 4, 2008, pp. 523–543. doi: 10.1080/00141840802563956.

Gallagher, Shaun, and Jonathan Cole. "Body Image and Body Schema in a deafferented subject." In *Body and Flesh: A Philosophical Reader*, edited by Donn Welton. Blackwell, 1998, pp. 131–147.

Gallese, V. "The Roots of Empathy and the Shared Manifold Hypothesis and the Neural Basis of Intersubjectivity." *Psychopathology*, vol. 36, no. 4, 2003, pp. 171–180.

———. "Mirror Neurons, Embodied Simulation, and the Neural Basis of Social Identification." *Psychoanalytic Dialogues*, vol. 19, 2009, pp. 519–536.

Gallese, V., and C. Sinigaglia. "What is so Special about Embodied Simulation?" *Trends in Cognitive Sciences*, vol. 15, no. 11, 2011, pp. 512–519.

Gallese, V., et al. "Action Recognition in the Premotor Cortex." *Brain*, vol. 199, no. 2, 1996, pp. 593–609.

Ghosh, M., editor and translator. *Nandikesvara's Abhinayadarpanam*. Manisha Granthalaya, 1975.

Ghurye, G. S., *Caste and Race in India*. Popular Prakashan, 1969.

Giddens, Anthony. *Modernity and Self-Identity: Self and Society in the Late Modern Age*. Stanford University Press, 1991.

———. *Sociology*. Polity Press, 2009.

Goffman, Erving. *The Presentation of the Self in Everyday Life*. Penguin, 1959.

Goldman, Alvin. *Simulating Minds: The Philosophy, Psychology and Neuroscience of Mindreading*. Oxford University Press, 2006.

Gough, Kathleen, and David M. Schneider, editors. *Matrinileal Kinship*. University of California Press, 1961.

Growtowski, J. *Towards a Poor Theater*. Simon & Shuster, 1968.

Guha, Sumit. *Beyond Caste: Identity and Power in South Asia, Past and Present*. Brill, 2013.

Hage, Ghasan. *White Nation*. Taylor and Francis, 2002.

Hallam, E., and T. Ingold. "Creativity and Cultural Improvisation: An Introduction." In *Creativity and Cultural Improvisation*, edited by E. Hallam and T. Gold. Berg, 2007, pp. 1–24.

Hapgood, Elizabeth R. *An Actor Prepares*. Lowe and Brydone (Printers) Limited, 1937.

Heidegger, Martin. *Being and Time*. Translated by John Macquarrie and Edward Robinson. Blackwell Publishers Ltd, 1973.

Hickok, Gregory. *The Myth of Mirror Neurons: The Real Neuroscience of Communication and Cognition.* WW Norton &Co, 2015.

Hodge, A. *Twentieth Century Actor Training.* Routledge, 2000.

Hopkins, Washburn E. "Hindu Salutations." *Hopkins: Bulletin of the School of Oriental Studies*, vol. 6, no. 2, 1931, pp. 369–383.

Hulton, Dorinda, and Kapsali, Maria. "Yoga and Stanislavski: Reflections on the Past and Applications for the Present and Furture." *Theater, Dance and Performance Training*, vol. 5, 2017, pp. 37–47.

Husserl, Edmund. *Formal and Transcendental Logic.* Martinus Nijhoff, 1969.

———. *General Introduction to Pure Phenomenology.* Routledge, 2012.

Ingold, Tim. "Culture on The Ground: The World Perceived Through the Feet." *Journal of Material Culture*, vol. 9, no. 3, 2004, pp. 315–340.

Iyer, Bharatha. *Kathakali; The Sacred Dance-Drama of Malabar.* Luzac and Company, 1955.

Iyer, Nithya. "Asian-Australian Theatre Baptizes Othello: The Magic Hour." *Peril*, 15 June 2016, http://peril.com.au/topics/arts/asian-australian-theatre-baptizes-othello-the-magic-hour. Accessed 25.06.2016.

Jeffrey, Robin. *The Decline of Nayar Dominance: Society and Politics in Travancore, 1847 - 1908.* University of Sussex Press, 1976.

Jones, Clifford R., and Betty True. *Kathakali: An Introduction to the Dance-Drama of Kerela.* Theater Arts Books, 1970.

Jortner, David, and Kathy Foler. "James R. Brandon." *Asian Theatre Journal*, vol. 28, no. 2, 2011, pp. 341–355.

Kalsi, Sewa Singh. *The Evolution of a Sikh Community in Britain: Religious and Social Change Among the Sikhs of Leeds and Bradford.* Leeds: University of Leeds, Dept. of Theology and Relgious Studies, 1992.

Kapila, Vatsyayan. *Indian Classical Dance.* Sangeet Natak Academy, 1974.

———. *Aesthetic Theories and Forms in Indian Tradition.* Munshiram Manoharlal, 2008.

Khare R. S., editor. *Caste, Hierarchy and Individualism.* OUP, 2006.

Khokar, Ashish. *Teacher & Guru.* Printways, 2016.

Kiernander, A. *Ariane Mnouchkine and the Theatre du Soleil.* Cambridge Universiy Press, 1993.

Kohler, E., et al. "Hearing Sounds, Understanding Actions: Action Representation in Mirror Neurons." *Science*, vol. 297, 2002, pp. 846–848.

Kothari, Sunil. *New Directions in Indian Dance.* Marg Publications, 2003.

Krishnamoorthy, K. *The Dhvanyaloka and Its Critics.* Kavyalaya Publishers, 1968.

———. *Studies in Indian Aesthetics and Criticism.* Mysore Printing and Publishing House, 1979.

Kumar, Pushpendra. *Natyasastra of Bharatamuni*, vol. 1–4. New Bharatiya Book Corporation, 2010.

Kumeiga, J. *The Theatre of Grotowski.* Methun, 1985.

Lan, Li Yong, and Kennedy Dennis. *Shakespeare in Asia: Contemporary Performance.* Cambridge University Press, 2010.

Landon-Smith, Kristine. "Towards an Intracultural Actor Training: Utilising the Cultural Context of the Performer." Dissertation, University of East London, 2016.

Leder, D. *The Absent Body.* University Press Chicago, 1990.

Ledger, Adam J. *Odin Teatre: Theater in a New Century.* Palgrave Macmillian, 2012.

Ledger, Adam K., et al. "The Question of Documentation: Creative Strategies in Performance Research." In *Research Methods in Theatre and Performance*, edited by Baz Kershaw and Helen Nicholson. Edinburgh University Press, 2011, pp. 162–185.

Lidova, Natalia. *Drama and Ritual of Early Hinduism*. Motilal Banarasi Das Publishers, 1994.

Lipner, Julis. *Hindus: Their Religious Beliefs and Practices*. Routledge, 2012.

Loomba, Ania. *'Local-Manufacture Made-in-India Othello Fellows': Issues of Race, Hybridity and Location in Post-Colonial Shakespeares*. *Post-colonial Shakespeares*. Edited by Ania Loomba and Martin Orkin. Routledge, 1998.

———. *A Companion to Shakespeare and Performance*. Edited by Barbara Hodgson and W.B. Worthen. Blackwell Publishing, 2005.

Madhavan, Arya. "Eyescape: Aesthetics of 'Seeing' in 'Kutiyattam.'" *Asian Theatre Journal*, vol. 29, no. 2, 2012, pp. 550–570.

Madhavan, A., and Nair, S. "The Kinetic Body: Foot Memory and Dispositions of the Body in Performance." In *Body and Performance: Ways of Being a Body*, edited by Sandra Reeve. Triarchy, 2013.

Mee, Erin. "'Rasa Is/As/And Emotional Contagion." In *Natyasastra: Aesthetics, Epistemology & Performance Practice. Editor Nair Sreenath.*. McFarland Press, 2014, pp. 157–168.

Menon, Dilip. "The Moral Community of the Teyyattam: Popular Culture in Late Colonial Malabar." *Studies in Social History*, vol. 9, 1993, pp. 187–216.

Menon, Narayana, et al. *Guru-Shishya Parampara: The Master Disciple Tradition in Classical Indian Dance and Music*. Arts Council of Great Britain, 1982.

Merleau, Ponty M. *Phenomenology of Perception*. Routledge & Kegan Paul, 1962.

———. *The Primacy of Perception*. Edited by James J. Edie. Northwestern University Press, 1964.

Merlin, B. *Beyond Stanislavski*. Nick Hern, 2001.

Meyrick, Julian. "Limits of Theory: Academic Versus Professional Understanding of Theatre Problems." *New Theatre Quarterly*, vol. 19, no. 3, 2003, pp. 230–242.

Mikkel, Bille, et al. *An Anthropology of Absence: Materializations of Transcendence and Loss*. Springer, 2010.

Morin, A. "Levels of Consciousness and Self-Awareness: A Comparison and Integration of Various Neurocognitive Views." *Consciousness and Cognition*, vol. 15, 2006, pp. 358–371.

Munsi Sarkar, Unmimala and Burridge Stephanie. *Traversing Tradition: Celebrating Dance in India*. Routledge, 2012.

Nair, D. Appukuttan, and Paniker Ayyappa K., editors. *Kathakali: The Art of the Non-Worldly*. Marg, 1993.

Nair, S. *Restoration of Breath Consciousness and Performance*. Brill, 2007.

———. *The Natyashastra and the Body in Performance*. Macfarland, 2015.

Narayanan, Mundoli. "Body Centric Knowledge: Traditions of Performance and Pedagogy in Kathakali." *Indian Journal of History of Science*, vol. 51, no. 1, 2016, pp. 231–242.

Nayar Prabodhchandran, V. R., et al. "Kalyanasaugandhikam (The Flower of Good Fortune), A Kathakali Drama." *Asian Theater Journal*, vol .13, no. 1, 1996, pp. 1–25.

Nelson, Robin. "Conceptual Frameworks for PaR and Related Pedagogy: From 'Hard Facts' to 'Liquid Knowing'." In *Practice as Research in the Arts: Principles, Protocols, Pedagogies, Resistances*. Palgrave Macmillan, 2013, pp. 49–70.

Osinski, Z. *Growtowski and His Laboratory*. Performing Arts Journal Publications, 1980.

Pandeya Avinash, C. *The Art of Kathakali*. Kitabistan, 1961.

Pavis, Patrice, editor. *The Intercultural Performance Reader*. Routledge, 1996.

Peterson, W. *Theater and the Politics of Culture in Singapore*. Wesleyen University Press, 2001.

———. "Being Affected: An Interview with Ong Keng Sen of TheatreWorks Singapore in Conversation with William Peterson." In *Theatre and Adaptation: Return, Rewrite, Repeat*, edited by Margherita Laera. Bloomsbury Methuen, 2014, pp. 165–180.

Piccini, Angela, and Baz Kershaw. "Practice as Research in Performance: From Epistemology to Evaluation." *Digital Creativity*, vol. 15, no. 2, 2004, pp. 86–92.

Pillai Evoor, Rajendran. *Personal Interviews*. 11 July 2016 and 26 August 2016.

Pitches, Jonathan. *Vsevolod Meyerhold*. Routledge, 2003.

Pitkow, Marlene Beth. *Representations of the Feminine in Kathakali: Dance-Drama of Kerala State, South India*. ProQuest Dissertations, 1998.

———. "The Good, the Bad and the Ugly: Kathakali's Females and the Men Who Play Them." In *Between Fame and Shame: Performing Women – Women Performers in India Part 3*, edited by Heidrun BrücknerHanne M. de Bruin and Heike Moser Harrassowitz Verlag, 2011, pp. 223–243.

Pollock, Sheldon. *A Rasa Reader*. Permanent Black, 2016.

Prickett, S. "Guru or Teacher? Shishya or Student? Pedagogic Shifts in South Asian Dance Training in India and Britain." *South Asia Research*, vol. 27, no. 1, 2007, pp. 25–41.

Raina, Arjun. *The Painted Devil*. Partridge, 2014.

———. "The Art of Creating a Kathakali Performer's 'Presence'." *Theater, Dance and Performance Training*, Taylor and Francis, vol. 6, no. 3, 2015, pp. 323–338.

———. "Kathakali Mirror Box." *Theater, Dance and Performance training*, Taylor and Francis, vol. 8, no. 1, 2017, pp. 61–74.

Raina, M. K. "Guru-Shishya Relationship in Indian Culture: The Possibility of a Creative Resilient Framework." *Psychology & Developing Societies*, vol. 14, no. 1, 2002, pp. 167–198.

Ram, Ronki. "Beyond Conversion and Sanskritisation: Articulating an Alternative Dalit Agenda in East Punjab." *Modern Asian Studies*, vol. 46, 2012, pp. 639–702. doi:10.1017/S0026749X11000254.

Ramachandran, V. S., and S. Blakeslee. *Phantoms in the Brain*. Fourth Estate, 1998.

Ramachandran, V. S., and D. Rogers-Ramachandran. "Synesthesia in Phantom Limbs Induced with Mirrors." *Proceedings of the Royal Society B*, 1996, vol. 29, pp. 377–86. doi: 10.1098/rspb.1996.0058.

Ramachandran, Vilayanur. "The Neurons That Shaped Civilization." *TED Talk*, November 2009, https://www.ted.com/talks/vs_ramachandran_the_neurons_that_shaped_civilization.

Richmond, Farley P. "Asian Theater Materials: A Selected Biography." *The Drama Review*, vol. 15, no. 2, 1971a, pp. 312–323.

———. "Some Religious Aspects of Indian Traditional Theatre." *The Drama Review*, vol. 15, no. 2, 1971b, pp. 123–131.

———. "The Political Role of Theatre in India." *Educational Theatre Journal*, vol. 25, no. 3, 1973, pp. 318–334.

———. "The Multiple Dimensions of Time and Space in Kutiyattam, the Sanskrit Theatre of Kerala." *Asian Theater Journal*, vol. 2, 1985, pp. 50–60.

———. "The Bhasa Festival Trivandrum, India." *Asia Theatre Journal*, vol. 6, no. 1, 1989, pp. 68–76.

Richmond, Farley P., et al. *Indian Theatre: Traditions of Performance*. Motilal Banarsidass, 1993.

Roy, Arundhati. *The God of Small Things*. Random House, 1997.

Sadasivan, N. S. *A Social History of India*. A. P. H. Publication, 2000.

Safwan, Amir. "History of Kathakali: Of Art, Agency, and Aesthetics." *Literophile*, vol. 7, no. 3, 2014, pp. 16–19.

Sapir, E. *Culture, Langage, and Personality, Selected Essays*. Edited by D. Mandelbaum. University of California Press, 1961.

Sebanz, N., et al. "Joint Action: Bodies and Minds Moving Together." *Trends in Cognitive Sciences*, vol. 10, no. 2, 2006, pp. 70–76.

Schechner, Richard. "A Reply to Rustom Bharucha." *Asian Theatre Journal*, vol. 1, no. 2, 1984, pp. 245–253.

———. *Between Theatre and Anthropology*. Routledge, 1985.

———. "The Five Avante Gardes or....... None?" In *The Twentieth Century Performance Reader*, 2nd edn, edited by Michael Huxley and Noel Witts. London: Routledge, 2002, pp. 7–17, 1993.

———. *Performance Theory*. Routledge, 1988.

Schechner, Richard, and Willa Appel, editors. *By Means of Performance: Intercultural Studies of Theatre and Ritual*. Press Syndicate of the University of Cambridge, 1990.

Scherer, K. R., and P. Ekman, editors. *Approaches to Emotion*. Lawrence Erlbaum Associates, 1984.

Scott, A. C. *Theatre in Asia*. Macmillan, 1972.

Shakespeare, S. W. *Othello*. Edited by J. A. E. Honigmann, and Arden Shakespeare, Thomas Learning, 2006.

Shawn, Ted. *Gods Who Dance*. E. P. Dutton, 1929.

Shulman, David. *More than Real: A History of the Imagination in South India*. Harvard University Press, 2012.

Shwartz, Susan L. *Rasa: Performing the Divine in India*. Columbia University Press, 2006.

Singh, Akhilesh Kumar. "When Brahmins Did Not Touch Mayawati's Feet." *Times of India*, 17 May 2007. https://timesofindia.indiatimes.com/india/When-Brahmins-did-not-touch-Mayawatis-feet/articleshow/2055822.cms. Accessed 25 June 2018.

Smith, Helen. *Personal Interview*. 30 June 2016.

Srinivas, M. N. "A Note on Sanskritization and Westernization." In *Caste in Modern India and Other Essays*. Asia Publishing House, 1962, pp. 42–62.

Srinivasan, Priya. *Sweating Saris: Indian Dance as Transnational Labor*. Temple University Press, 2011.

Strathern, Andrew J. *Body Thoughts*. University of Michigan Press, 1996.

Taylor, Diana. *The Archive and the Repertoire: Performing Cultural Memory in the Americas*. Duke University Press, 2003.

Thapar, Romila. *Interpreting Early India*. Oxford University Press, 1992.

Thomas, Terence. "Old Allies, New Neighbors: Sikhs in Britain." In *The Growth of Religious Diversity: Britain from 1945*, Vol 1, edited by Gerald Parsons. Abingdon, UK: Open University/Routledge, 1993, pp. 205–242.

Trowsdale, Jo, and R. Hayhow. "Psycho-Physical Theatre Practice as Embodied Learning for Young People with Learning Disabilities." *International Journal of Inclusive Education*, vol. 19, no. 10, 2015, pp. 1022–1036. doi: 10.1080/13603116.2015.1031832.

Tsakiris, M., et al. "Having a Body Versus Moving Your Body: How Agency Structures Body-Ownership." *Consciousness and Cognition*, vol. 15, 2006, pp. 423–432.

———. "On Agency and Body-Ownership: Phenomenological and Neurocognitive Reflections." *Consciousness and Cognition*, vol. 16, 2007, pp. 645–660.

Turner, Jane. *Eugenio Barba*. Routledge, 2004.

Umlita, M. A., et al. "I Know What You Are Doing: A Neurophysicological Study." *Neuron*, vol. 32, 2001, pp. 91–101.

Varley, J. "Sanjukta Panigrahi Dances for The Gods." *New Theatre Quarterly*, vol. XIV, no. 55, 1998, pp. 249–273.

Wallace, Dace. "The Concept of Rasa in Sanskrit Dramatic Theory." *Educational Theatre Journal*, vol. 15, no. 3, 1963, pp. 249–254.

Wallace, Lori Lee. *The Intercultural and Psychophysical Acting Pedagogy of Phillip Zarrilli*. UMI Dissertation Publishing Michigan, 2012.

Watson, I. "Odin Teatret: "The Million" La Mama Annex, New York, April 26." *The Drama Review*, vol. 29, no. 3, 1985, pp. 131–137.

———. *Negotiating Cultures: Eugenio Barba and the Intercultural Debate*. Manchester University Press, 2002.

Zarrilli, P. *The Kathakali Complex, Actor, Performance & Structure*. Abhinav Publications, 1984.

———. "Contested Narratives On and Off the *Kathakali* Dance-Drama Stage." *Modern Drama*, vol. 35, no. 1, 1992, pp. 101–116.

———. *Kathakali Dance-Drama Where Gods and Demons Play*. Routledge, 2000a.

———. "Embodying the Lion's 'Fury'." *Performance Research: A Journal of the Performing Arts*, vol. 5, no. 2, 2000b, pp. 41–54.

———. "Towards a Phenomenological Model of the Actor's Embodied Modes of Experience." *Theatre Journal*, vol. 56, no. 4, 2004, pp. 653–666.

———. *Psychophysical Acting: An Intercultural Approach after Stanislavski*. Routledge, 2009. DVD-ROM by Peter Hulton.

———. "Psychophysical Approaches and Practices in India: Embodying Processes and States of 'Being–Doing'." *New Theatre Quarterly*, vol. 27, 2011, pp. 244–271. doi:10.1017/S0266464X11000455.

Zarrilli, P., et al. *Acting: Psychophysical Phenomenon and Process: Intercultural and Interdisciplinary Perspectives*. Palgrave Macmillan, 2013.

Zoete, Beryl de, and Walter Spies. *Dance and Drama in Bali*. Oxford University Press, 1938.

Index